MW01518169

Every Day I'm Married

The Importance of Being Intentional about Every Moment

Marcus Huff

ISBN 979-8-88616-553-1 (paperback)
ISBN 979-8-88616-554-8 (digital)

Christian Faith Publishing
832 Park Avenue
Meadville, PA 16335
www.christianfaithpublishing.com

Printed in the United States of America

This book could not have been possible without God's help and guidance. I dedicate this book to my lifelong coauthor, partner in ministry for life, and wife, Anjala. To my children Brooklynn, Sean, and Riley, there is nothing you can't do, and I am proud of whom you are becoming. Thanks to all the love and support received from my family, friends, and loved ones.

Marcus Huff

CONTENTS

This book centers on the belief that it's not a certain milestone you have to accomplish in your marriage, but it's understanding every moment matters.

PREFACE

I pray this book uniquely ministered to each person whether single and seeking a relationship, engaged to be married, or married for some time as only God can do. God birthed the idea for this book almost six years ago while my wife and I were over the marriage ministry at our church. I witnessed so many differences, and at the same time, so many similarities listening to others share their marriage experiences.

While listening to both the men and women, what stood out to me was the men's perspective. It was different and unique. The men tended to view marriage through a singular and, at times, stereotypical *masculine lens*. I have been asked who this book is for and the audience I believe I am addressing. I believe this book is for both wives and husbands, encouraging and challenging them both, but my perspective is from a husband. My prayer is although wives can gain insight as to how their husbands think, this book is intended to speak to husbands worldwide and for generations to come. You are not the only ones going through and experiencing the things you are going through. Even now, there is hope for you to become better, do better, and be better in every moment of your marriage and life.

INTRODUCTION

"I need a moment." These words were said to me by my wife after I urged her to continue a conversation too hard. This was the first year of our marriage.

Have you ever said those words before or felt like you needed to say this to somebody else? Maybe your spouse, a loved one, coworker, child, or honestly, given the right moment, you can insert anyone's name. When my wife and I first got married, it felt like she was constantly saying this to me. Now I admit, I can be stubborn and sometimes a pusher to resolve an issue right away; but early in my marriage, I felt like I heard "I need a moment" from my wife a lot.

Before I go further, let me introduce myself because I can feel the pending judgment through the pages. My name is Marcus Huff. I don't have a million followers or even thousands on social media. I currently work a nine-to-five, and you can find me taking my kids to their various sports practices and completing a *honey-do* project around the house.

I am originally from Michigan, and I grew up middle class with both parents, two younger sisters, and an older brother. My mom and dad both worked, and although I did not have everything I wanted, I had everything I needed. We were a hand-me-down family, which simply means my new clothes were my brother's old clothes. My parents have been married for thirty-seven years and counting. I went to the University of Michigan (Go Blue!) for college and met my wife at a party. We danced all night long and after the party lost touch. We reconnected sometime later and became close friends. We got married after graduating college and had our first child a few years later.

We were young when we first married. I am letting you know about me because I am no different from your neighbor, and I invite you in this book to journey with me on navigating the struggles, challenges, joys, and blessings of day-by-day, moment-by-moment marriage.

I am not perfect. I love my wife of fifteen years and our three children unconditionally. I strive every moment to be the best husband and father I believe God is calling me to be. This book is not a secret marriage formula to practice daily, giving you the perfect marriage. If I were to take all the chapters of this book and summarize them into one paragraph, that paragraph into one sentence, and that sentence into one word, for me that word is *moment*. Even though divorce rates are at an all-time high, things that lead to a decision to separate from your spouse are typically due to several different culminating moments, not just one. If a series of negative moments can lead to negative consequences, then by principle, a series of positive moments can lead to positive outcomes. You truly reap what you sow as found in scripture.

Galatians 6:7 (NIV) states, "Do not be deceived, God is not mocked; for whatever a man sows, that he will also reap."

This book gives insight into my life lessons through biblical principles. I believe in being intentional about each moment you have. I am a certified marriage counselor, have served in the marriage ministry, seen and witnessed marriages in all different stages, ranging from madly in love to deciding to divorce. We all need help in this journey of marriage because it requires work. This book is focused on providing a different perspective on maximizing each moment—day, month, year, and beyond—with your spouse and your marriage.

When my wife and I led the couples' ministry, one of the most powerful times was gathering and sharing experiences. To know that your marriage is not the only one going through what you are going through helped us in our marriage. The goal, if you hang until the end, is for your perspective to change how you not only view your marriage but how you view yourself. No matter who you are and what you are going through, make a commitment to read this book with an open heart and receptive mind, trusting God to do the rest.

Please note that although my perspective is biblically based, the information shared is principal knowledge. Accepting every belief shared in this book is not required. The goal and hope are that this book speaks to you in ways to help your marriage or relationship in whatever stage you are in.

I hope my perspective challenges you to fulfill the purpose you were called for in marriage and in life. Let the journey begin.

CHAPTER 1

Every Moment I'm Married

*Life is available only in the present moment. If
you abandon the present moment, you cannot
live the moments of your daily life deeply.*

—Thích Nhất Hạnh

The moments that led to this book

When Anjala and I first got married in 2007, people used to tell
us, "If you can make it through the first year of marriage, you will
be all right." We also heard if you could make it through the third,
fifth, seventh, and tenth year of marriage, your marriage will make
it. At the time, I optimistically would hear the Destiny's Child song
playing in my head, "I'm a Survivor, I'm going to make it, I won't
stop, I will work harder," me nodding my head, thinking, *Anjala and
I got this. We are survivors.* Imagine if that is all it took for a successful
marriage; just staying together for a certain number of years with the
confidence that in time, your marriage will eventually work out. We
waited year after year for that moment to arrive, but it never came for
us. In fact, our early years of marriage were challenging.

To give context, we were married in our early twenties. I pro-
posed senior year of college, and we were married the following year.
Did I mention that we were both very stubborn in addition to being

married young by today's standards? I struggled in our early years of marriage with being self-centered, selfish, and insecure. We would argue about little things, get into it over nothing, and even go days at a time without speaking at all. Ironically, we struggled through our first, third, and seventh years of marriage. I will talk about our *seventh* year later, but a moment from that year was a turning point for how I viewed my role in our marriage. In reflection, I wonder how much better I would have navigated some of the challenges I experienced if I had someone who provided me with marriage guidance *before* I was married and *during* my marriage.

From countless conversations with other married couples, I have learned that our challenges are not unique. Other marriages may not be experiencing the same thing, but as Solomon said in **Ecclesiastes 1:9 (NIV), "What has been will be again, what has been done will be done again; there is nothing new under the sun."** The constant struggle to figure out how to navigate marriage inspired me to get my thoughts out, but the moments experienced leading marriage ministry at my church pushed me to write. I recall one session where a couple described the same situation but from different perspectives. It was tough to watch. Not because it was uncomfortable, but because in some ways, it was familiar. The wife was sure she was right and so was the husband. It seemed like the session focused on who could prove it the most. It was as if they were two lawyers in a courtroom, and the couple's ministry was the jury.

It's understandable to disagree or have differing opinions. However, when that difference is driving a wedge between you and your spouse, it is unhealthy, and the struggle is obvious to those who are bystanders. Has this ever been you? Have you been the couple before that has allowed private misalignment and understanding to spill over into the public?

I believe the Word of God is full of all the answers we need for marriage, but you don't hear a lot of biblical examples from scripture on married couples. First and foremost, in your marriage, the standard of love you show your spouse needs to be greater than you! It is difficult to show your spouse something you have limited experience in or have been shaped by poor past experiences. The Bible provides that standard. *First Corinthians 13:1–13 (NLT) says:*

> *If I could speak all the languages of earth and of angels, but didn't love others, I would only be a noisy gong or a clanging cymbal. If I had the gift of prophecy, and if I understood all of God's secret plans and possessed all knowledge, and if I had such faith that I could move mountains, but didn't love others, I would be nothing. If I gave everything I have to the poor and even sacrificed my body, I could boast about it; but if I didn't love others, I would have gained nothing. Love is patient and kind. Love is not jealous or boastful or proud or rude. It does not demand its own way. It is not irritable, and it keeps no record of being wronged. It does not rejoice about injustice but rejoices whenever the truth wins out. Love never gives up, never loses faith, is always hopeful, and endures through every circumstance. Prophecy and speaking in unknown languages and special knowledge will become useless. But love will last forever! Now our knowledge is partial and incomplete, and even the gift of prophecy reveals only part of the whole picture! But when the time of perfection comes, these partial things will become useless. When I was a child, I spoke and thought and reasoned as a child. But when I grew up, I put away childish things. Now we see things imperfectly, like puzzling reflections in a mirror, but then we will see everything with perfect clarity. All that I know now is partial and incomplete, but then I will know everything completely, just as God now knows me completely. Three things will last forever—faith, hope, and love—and the greatest of these is love.*

3

I love the entire chapter, but I particularly view the fifteen standards found in verses four through seven as God's standard of love for building a loving and lasting marriage. They are like a checklist that I have internalized and reflected on daily. I default to this list when I find myself off track. I have honestly struggled with every one of the items on this list. They have stretched me, required work, and have set the bar so high to achieve that I cannot do it without God's help, thus a primary reason to establish a relationship with God through Jesus.

Someone can spend a lifetime just trying to become a more patient person or learning not to keep a record of wrongs. Imagine trying to fulfill just five items, let alone all fifteen. Even if you never capture them all, checking as many boxes as you can is certainly worth it, and I would say necessary. We are still in the first chapter, but

> ...no matter where you are in your marriage,
> believe and declare, "Your marriage is worth it!"

Go ahead; I know people may be around, but by faith declare, "MY MARRIAGE IS WORTH IT!" If you can't say it, then you can't believe it. If you don't believe it, then you can't live it.

Although there are varying standards for love, I want to challenge you to join me in using God's standard of love in your marriage. Again, it starts with knowing and accepting God because I believe he is the only one capable of keeping your marriage. If you are experiencing challenges, God can turn your marriage around or help you to find and prepare for the one God has purposed in your life. Below is a checklist developed from 1 Corinthians 13:4–7 to conduct a self-assessment of where you currently measure in expressing love. This is a self-assessment, so be honest with yourself. Take this moment to mark whether you feel you meet God's standard of love, are in progress, or know you need to work more on or be more intentional with a certain love characteristic.

THE LOVE CHECKLIST		MEETS STANDARD	IN PROGRESS	NEEDS WORK
1.	Patient			
2.	Kind			
3.	Not Jealous			
4.	Not Boastful			
5.	Not Proud			
6.	Not Rude			
7.	Not Selfish			
8.	Not Irritable			
9.	Keeps No Record of Wrong			
10.	Does Not Rejoice in Evil			
11.	Rejoices in Truth			
12.	Never Gives Up			
13.	Never Loses Faith			
14.	Always Hopeful			
15.	Endures Every Circumstance			

Throughout this book, there will be moments of prayer or communicating your heart to God. I believe that prayer to God can change things, and I ask that you by faith pray these prayers with me.

Simple prayer: Father, thank you for simply revealing your standard of love. You know our hearts and the plans you have for us before we were even born. In areas where we meet the standard, help us to grow in greater grace in this area. In areas of progress, help us not be weary in doing well while making progress. In areas that we need work, help us not get discouraged, but cast our cares onto you knowing you care as we believe your strength is made perfect in our weakness. In Jesus's name, amen!

Enjoying the good moments

What is a moment? *Merriam-Webster* defines a moment as "a portion or point of time, an instant." Our lives are full of a series of points in time, resulting in a collection of impactful or uneventful moments. A moment in life should not be taken for granted because it can never be returned or relived. Moments in life matter, and I am learning to value each one because one moment can change your life forever.

I remember the moment I asked my wife, Anjala, to marry me. We had been dating for about a year after being best friends the year before. I scheduled a date day and recorded the day on video. I recorded every activity, from stopping by her apartment and cooking her breakfast to taking her ice-skating. We concluded that evening in my apartment with our friends, family, food, and dessert. We were surrounded by people we loved and who loved us. Before we ate, I gathered everyone in a small circle like the ones you use to gather for in elementary school, and I prayed over the food. While her eyes were still closed, I broke from the circle and began to thank God for the blessing she had been in my life, and my prayer transitioned into a proposal. Anjala stood there, still with her eyes closed in prayer, until I grabbed her hand. When she opened her eyes, I was on one knee proposing. It was unexpected. It was special. That was a life-changing moment, and everything was captured on video.

I remember our wedding day being especially significant. On June 23, 2007, we were married in Muskegon, Michigan, by Anjala's bishop and spiritual father, Bishop Nathaniel Wells Jr. We were wed in the church she grew up in, surrounded by family and friends, and followed by good food and great reception. We went on a cruise to Mexico for our honeymoon, enjoying the sun, eating whatever we wanted, and enjoying each other as newlyweds. Our wedding and honeymoon were great moments!

Our oldest child was a miracle birth. I was in DC at a work event when Anjala went into labor. I immediately left the event and headed to the airport to catch a flight. It was like a scene out of a movie, as I went from airline to airline trying to catch a flight. I made it on a plane and to the hospital in time to see my daughter be born. This was an unbelievable moment.

Our oldest child was two years old and my wife was twenty weeks pregnant when we experienced another one of these moments. Anjala took every precaution and faithfully went to all her doctor's appointments. On this day, she had a routine ultrasound appointment expecting to find out the sex of our new baby. The doctor asked the typical questions and walked us through what she would be doing. She touched my wife's stomach for two seconds when she pulled back the ultrasound equipment. Both Anjala and I stared at her. She paused and asked if we were there to find out the sex of our baby. My wife looked confused and confirmed with a slow, "Yes." Hesitantly, the doctor said, "Oh. Well, there are two babies."

I was shocked, and Anjala was laughing in disbelief. She was twenty weeks along, and she hardly looked pregnant. In fact, very few people knew she was pregnant at that time. The doctor checked again and said, "You all are having twins." This was a significant and life-changing moment that we will never forget.

Reflector or deflector

As I look back, these were all great, amazing, and unforgettable moments to start our marriage. But if you are honest, the joy of these moments does not always last. ***Ecclesiastes 3:1 (KJV) says, "To everything there is a season, and a time to every purpose under the heaven."*** I have learned that you can't always stay in good and happy moments. Trials and tribulations in marriage will come but in a way, they have to. Without trials and tribulations, where would growth come from? If a seed that is buried in the ground does not die, how can it ever grow? My wife and I have had good moments, but it would not have strengthened our marriage if we never struggled through tough moments. Your response in the not-so-good moments of life can determine your longevity in marriage.

Are you a reflector or deflector? During struggles in your marriage, is it usually your spouse's fault? Do you find yourself questioning, after all these years, why they still don't understand you? "They knew who I was when we got married, I don't get why they are acting like everything is brand new now. I have to do everything myself because they mess everything up. Why didn't they think about that happening and plan accordingly?"

If you have stated anything like this, you may tend to deflect when struggles arise, looking at the fault of others. Jesus said this in *Matthew 7:3–5 (NLT):*

> *And why worry about a speck in your friend's eye when you have a log in your own? How can you think of saying to your friend, 'Let me help you get rid of that speck in your eye,' when you can't see past the log in your own eye? Hypocrite! First get rid of the log in your own eye; then you will see well enough to deal with the speck in your friend's eye.*

Being a *deflector* only looks at what the other person is or is not doing. It can limit your perspective and cause you to feel falsely empowered toward behaviors that are not helpful for the long-term health of your marriage and relationships.

Another response to trials, tribulations, and struggles is being a *reflector*. This is someone who looks at themselves during a struggle to determine what their role was during the situation. Like someone looking in a mirror, they reflect on the discussion or experience and say things like, "I wish I would have said something different to my spouse. Why do I get so angry when they say that to me? Lord, do a work in me. Help me be less and less stubborn and more and more patient. How can I be a better listener?"

Reflection is a vehicle that can drive to growth while *deflection* is a vehicle that can drive to isolation. Think back on your past relationships and assess whether you have been a deflector or reflector in the past. Can you see your choices impacted the type of relationships you have had in your life? Again, be honest with yourself when reflecting. The truth makes you free and positions you to give things you have struggled with to God for him to do work in you.

Simple prayer: Father, thank you for your patience with me. Help me to not deflect but reflect on situations that lead toward growing and becoming better and not complacent with who I have always been. I trust that you have ordered my steps, and please lead me down the path that strengthens my marriage and not isolates it. In Jesus's name, amen!

Understanding every moment is a lesson

When we first got married, Anjala and I were not making much money. We lived in a two-bedroom, one-bath apartment. We didn't have a lot of furniture and needed to purchase a much-needed desk. This desk was the kind that had hundreds of pieces and multiple pages of instructions to assemble. It was our first building project together as newlyweds, and I was excited to put the desk together with my newly committed partner in life. Now our approach to building was completely different. Anjala is one for reading and following instructions, and I lean more on glancing at instructions but building based upon the picture. In other words, she had her way of putting it together, and I had mine. It was a disaster of a project. We found ourselves arguing and arguing about whose way was best. We fussed and were equally frustrated over the best way to put this desk together. What should have taken an hour or two took over a half day's work because we could not get on the same page. That moment in hindsight reflected our growing communication style early in our marriage. It was the progressive transition from communicating kindly and complimentarily in the *honeymoon phase* to impatient and a strong desire to get our individual points across.

Amos 3:3 (NLT) states, "Do two walk together unless they have agreed to do so?" As the scripture in Amos 3:3 questions, walking with someone comes from a place of *agreement*. Have you ever had to walk with someone you particularly didn't want to? It makes for an uncomfortable time together. There may be some pleasantries exchanged but even those are forced. Agreeing to walk with someone is agreeing to bring your entire emotional, mental, physical, and spiritual self to go from one place with someone to another.

Early in my marriage, I did not appreciate how a negative conversation or continuous sarcastic exchanges built up and contributed to learning to walk negatively together. People are creatures of habit, and if you learn to walk with someone out of a place of irritation, sarcasm, or frustration, this in turn will become the pace you set for every journey you take. Now I am not saying that every journey together is amazing, happy, and joyful; but being positively intentional about each moment can help develop habits that make the journey more enjoyable.

Sometimes verses like Amos 3:3 sound good but are hard to accomplish. I cannot emphasize enough; each moment in life has significance, particularly in our relationships and certainly in your marriage. We tend to focus on huge things in life, but the little moments every day have the potential to make lasting impacts on our marriage, both present and future.

Early in our relationship, when we were dating, Anjala used to love to lay down on my chest as we relaxed or watched a movie. It would be sporadic as if comfort and peace were at the center of the cuddle and embrace. One time, I was irritated by something she had done. As she was lying on me, it started to get uncomfortable. I tried to hold out without saying anything but ended up asking her if she could move off me in a not-so-friendly way. In that moment of frustration, it changed her laying on me in the same way to this day. She will still lay on me from time to time but not how she used to. I honestly don't think it's intentional, and maybe it is just me, but sometimes I think back and wonder if she no longer lays on me the same way because of that moment. Who knows if this is the case, but the point is that one moment can impact your future in ways you never fully realize.

It's like dropping a small stone in a pond of water. There are ripples created on the surface of the water. Depending on the size of the stone, the bigger the stone thrown, the bigger the ripples. To take it even further, we cannot see the impact the stone makes on the environment below the water. Similarly, smaller moments may not appear to impact us on the surface as much as a bigger moment in our marriages. However, enough smaller moments over time, just like stones thrown in a pond, will eventually impact the environment you can't see—your heart.

Have you gotten into a habit of speaking negatively to your husband or wife? Do you tend to lose patience easily when your spouse says something you find irritating? We tend to look for *the big stone* moments that trigger why you are so irritated or bothered when they do or say something a certain way. Maybe it is not one big moment but a series of little moments that you are unaware has impacted you.

Building together during tough moments

In the book of Genesis chapter two, verse twenty-four, God says something profound. ***Genesis 2:24 (KJV) tells us, "Therefore shall a man leave his father and his mother and shall cleave unto his wife: and they shall be one flesh."*** Leave and cleave to become one flesh. Early in my marriage, sex and intimacy were the only lenses I used to view this scripture. My perspective on this verse has changed in the past fifteen years of marriage. Focusing on the *oneness* more than my immature perspective of intimacy. I've learned the more my wife and I are on one accord, on the same page, constructively working through problems, or in essence, behaving as one flesh, the more I see myself in our interactions. When I can place a check in a new area from our love standard checklist, the more I see myself and not just my wife in our marriage.

The problem early on in my marriage is that my standard of love was based upon songs, movies, experiences, commercials, and other non-biblical principles. If she was not living up to the standard I developed, she was the problem of my irritation. I was justified in my own eyes because of the confidence I had in my experiences and perspective, but when I committed to God's standard of loving my spouse, it allowed me to see myself more clearly against the standard God set and not my own. ***Proverbs 21:2 (NLT) says, "People may be right in their own eyes, but the Lord examines their heart."***

For example, 1 Corinthians 13:5 says love is not easily irritable. This scripture helps me identify times when I am easily irritable with my spouse. I want to calm down, and I am watching myself saying, "Calm down," but my body and mind are not listening. Since I know this about myself, I try to prepare for these moments by walking away from the conversation when I get too emotional or not talking for a moment until I can calm down. The important thing is to start to see yourself based upon God's standard of love and not your own. Being self-reflective has been extremely helpful, and you must be able to see yourself and be accountable for yourself and not just the wrong you see in your spouse. Questions that help me to be more self-reflective are as follows:

1) How could I have said that differently?
2) How could I have said that with more kindness and patience?
3) How do I keep calm during heated discussions?
4) Do I always need to be right?
5) Why did I get so upset?
6) Is getting that point across more important than making my marriage work?
7) Am I only focused on what they said, and have I considered what I said?

The moment you realize iron sharpens iron

I'm not saying you always need to be together physically, but I believe that absence makes the heart grow founder. Regardless of your perspective, when you are together, make it count. When my wife and I are together, we have fun, watch movies, or binge on TV series. But we also take time to discuss our goals, go over our finances, pray, study God's Word, and sharpen each other. ***Proverbs 27:17 (NIV) states, "As iron sharpens iron, so one person sharpens another."*** The sharpening process often comes in tough conversations about what we will do with our finances, how we plan to spend vacation this year, or what activities the kids will be involved in. These may sound like simple things, but they can be tough conversations that have led to someone breaking or feeling broken by the other's communication style.

The process of sharpening iron is grinding away worn and abrasive metals with a tool that is harder or as hard as the tool itself. Sharpening is a process of refining, polishing, smoothing, and correcting. You can't get to the latter phase without chipping away at the older you. We often go into marriage with the disposition that I am who I am and will never change. We can find ourselves saying to our friends when we are *striking metal against metal* or getting into an argument or disagreement, "He knew who I was when he married me" or "She knew what I was about, so I don't understand why they are acting different now." Neither one of you are the same person you were when you first met or even the same person you were yesterday. With each moment, your perspective changes, evolves, and adjusts into the person you are becoming. Staying who you were is a disservice to your spouse and your marriage. The goal should be growing together, sharpening each other until death do you part.

One of my favorite but challenging passages of scripture is in John 15 when Jesus talks about being the true vine and we are the branches. Jesus says that he cuts off every branch that does not produce fruit and prunes the branches that do bear fruit. To me, I understand cutting off the branches in my life of doubt, anxiety, worry, and jealousy that are not producing fruit; please take those away from me. But cutting back the joy, confidence, hope, faith, and love to name a few growing in my life doesn't seem to make sense to me naturally. God showed me in scripture that when he prunes or cuts back the fruit I possess, it is not intended to stop me from producing it but so that I can produce even more joy, confidence, hope, faith, and love. Interestingly, fruit is not for the tree or the branch to enjoy but for others to enjoy.

In other words, I need God to continue to prune areas in my life that don't belong so that I am constantly producing more and more faith, love, patience, hope, encouragement, support, and the list goes on for my wife, family, ministry, and others to feed from. That's another way we sharpen each other. She allows God to prune her, and I allow him to prune me, and in return, over time, we sharpen each other by being a constant source of strength and nourishment for our marriage.

Iron is tough and strong, which is a complementary trait in a partner. The only thing able to sharpen iron is something of equal or slightly greater strength. If it is too weak, it will not be able to sharpen; and if it is too strong, it could break. The moment you realize you are your partner's greatest advocate, encourager, lifter, strength, and support is when you start to behave that way. You may not control your spouse's behavior, but you can control whom God makes you.

Anjala and I are very competitive, and we can get lost in the spirit of competition. One time, we played basketball with the kids in the yard, and we got so competitive that it was a bit more aggressive than what the kids were used to seeing from us. The way we played, a referee would have called foul, and it ultimately discouraged one of my kids from wanting to play anymore. This may happen but make sure your children see the apology. Like I said, I am not perfect but striving for perfection. I know that's pretty bad, and God is still working on us, but in the competition of life, I am the first to push her dreams, ambitions, drives, and aspirations. We are partners and have made a commitment to do this together.

Every moment matters

I am constantly seeking to improve and be a better husband, father, and neighbor to others in my marriage. Aiming to become better and doing so are entirely different. Having a desire to change is essential, but how do you start the process? Becoming a better person in a moment started with me trying to be a better person in general. I just wanted to be better. I was tired of being snappy, sarcastic, and easily angered over little things. Tired of the comfort of stubbornness and settling with making it work. I wanted more from God and my marriage. Having this realization and honest moment helped me tremendously. It's like having an internal drive to do something. If your internal drive to change is not there for you, when the zeal is gone and the moment passes or you perceive your spouse or situation has pushed your button the wrong way, you will default back to the comfort of who you were and not whom you are trying to be.

> Victories are not always won on the battlefield
> but also in the moments before the battle.

King David is notoriously known for defeating Goliath, but that did not happen because he had a lucky moment on the battlefield. This victory was a result of trusting God in all the moments before the battle. In 1 Samuel 17:33, King Saul questioned if David could win this moment. David confidently spoke about how God helped him win moments in his past, and the same God that helped him win those moments would be the same God to help him win this moment. I believe God uses little moments to confirm whether we can handle bigger moments. *Luke 16:10 (NLT) tells us, "If you are faithful in little things, you will be faithful in large ones. But if you are dishonest in little things, you won't be honest with greater responsibilities."*

You have been asking for more patience, and you find yourself in an unexpected traffic jam on the way to an important meeting. You have been asking God to help with anger, and someone disrespects you publicly. You have been asking God to show you who is for you, and friends are no longer returning your calls. Every moment matters! I need God not just for the big moments in my marriage but for every moment. I have learned that the little moments build character and allow God to see if he can trust me in both little and bigger moments.

Are you trusting God in the smaller moments of your life? Those moments when no one else is around, and it's just you and God. One of my favorite passages is *1 Peter 5:7 (KJV), "Cast your cares upon God for He cares for you."* Are you trusting God to take your *anger, anxiety, cares, concerns, jealousy, problems, selfishness, stub-*

bornness, worries, unforgiveness, insert your specific concern here, and no longer carry the burden of trying to change on your own? God is concerned about what we are concerned about, so feel confident knowing you can take every moment to him. He cares about it all. If you are struggling with something in your marriage, give it to God right now; like seriously speak it out loud, and trust God to take that care from you onto himself. Trust him to work on this for you and start to recognize the moments when you are tested with what you spoke. Don't downplay any moment in your marriage and treat them all with the trust that God can help you through it.

Simple prayer: Father, thank you for each moment you have created. Let this chapter be the first step toward a changed perspective and approach to our marriage and relationships. Please help us live each moment intentionally, trusting you are in control. Let the journey for each relationship be graced with purpose and aimed at helping us to become what you created us to be. Thank you for this moment and for everything you have already done. In Jesus's name, amen!

CHAPTER 2

Every Day I'm Married

*This is a wonderful day, I have
never seen this before.*

—*Maya Angelou*

Do you remember the day?

Do you remember when you first started dating? Everything
was so exciting. You wanted to talk to your new love all the time.
When I first started dating Anjala, we would talk for hours at a time,
but we made sure to usually have those conversations after 9:00 p.m.
You see, back in my day, we were only allowed a certain amount of
minutes each month. If you went over those minutes, your phone bill
would be sky-high. After paying way too much on cell phone bills,
we switched to talking primarily when we had free minutes—after
9:00 p.m. My wife and I used to be on the phone for hours into the
night and early into the morning talking about nothing and everything simultaneously. A day was far too long to go without talking.

Taking it back even further, do you remember when you first
met your spouse? Who spoke first? Were you smooth or kind of
nervous? Maybe you danced the night away like us. Whatever your
story, each meeting, conversation, or interaction is unique and carries
the DNA of your relationship and marriage.

Deoxyribonucleic acid or DNA is the chemical name for the molecule that carries genetic instructions for all living things. DNA consists of two strands of various phosphate and sugar that wind around one another to form a shape known as a double helix. It's interesting these two strands carry similar things and are bound together continuously making us who we are. To me, that reflects our relationships. We are two individuals carrying similar but unique things, bound together to make it work emotionally, mentally, physically, and spiritually.

Similar to DNA, do you know what binds you together? Are you sure of the purpose of your marriage? It can be arguments, drugs, family, friends, money, people, sex, or sometimes even religion. If that bonding agent goes away or dies, then there becomes a strain on what's holding you together. My wife and I have learned that making God our bonding agent has helped us stay bound together when we did not want to be. ***Ecclesiastes 4:12 (NIV) says, "Though one may be overpowered, two can defend themselves. A cord of three strands is not quickly broken."*** Is God the third cord binding your marriage together?

What a difference a day makes

I once did an exercise where I wrote down everything I had to accomplish in my day. It included work tasks, taking care of the kids, and even a few obligated items lingering out there like going to the dentist. I had one or two things on my *honey-do list*, and finally, I managed to fit in one thing for me personally. Maybe you are like me and have a million things on your plate. Let me help you out. ***Proverbs 11:1 (KJV) states, "A false balance is an abomination to the Lord: but a just weight is his delight."*** There are few things that God says is an abomination to him. To know that not properly balancing your life is on that list messed me up in college. It still convicts me at times now when I am not properly prioritizing my time. I can have the best intentions of doing something, but if I am not intentional about making it a priority, it will not happen. I am learning that you can want your marriage or relationships to work, but if they are not a priority each day, marriage will be difficult.

As previously referenced, **Genesis 2:24 (NASB) says, "For this reason a man shall leave his father and his mother, and be joined to his wife; and they shall become one flesh."**

> Marriage is not about one person but two people getting past their individual plans to agree that their collective agenda is greater than their solo agendas.

Are you so focused on what you have going on that you simply miss checking in on your spouse to see how their day is going? When was the last time you took an emotional, mental, physical, or spiritual health day? When my wife and I are out of sync or I am not taking the appropriate amount of time for myself, it impacts my day more than I realize. If we are truly one, as Genesis 2:24 states, then when she is off, I am off. When she is hurting, I am hurting. When she is praised, then I am praised.

Selfishness can be hard to recognize. It is often a mask hiding an unyielding attitude, stubbornness, or being unbendable. Whenever you are wearing a mask, you are concealing some part of yourself. Maybe you're hiding insecurities or fear of losing power. Maybe you're scared of losing yourself. Maybe, like me, you are avoiding dealing with your own faults. When things got challenging early in our marriage, I would pray to God for him to change Anjala. What I realized when I matured was I really needed him to change me. So I changed my prayers from "God change Anjala" to "Bless my wife and change anything in me that is keeping me from being my best for you, my wife, family, and others."

Again, if the two of us are one, I should never be praying anything but blessings over my spouse even when we disagree because I recognize that when she's blessed, I am blessed. Don't let the mask of selfishness cause you to build character traits that could be harmful to your marriage. Instead, be intentional about wanting the best for your spouse and your marriage.

Building each day intentionally

My wife and I recently signed up for a gym membership. We get up early in the morning and work out together. After each workout, one of us will ask, "How was your workout?" The response is usually "Painful," "Good," "I didn't feel like doing it," or sometimes "I was tired during the workout." Being disciplined to get up early in the morning is difficult in itself. When you add leaving the house, going out in the cold, and putting your body through a little pain, it can be brutal. We both realized that we are building our bodies and health with each workout, and building it takes work. Work does not always feel good or pleasant or makes us happy, but the investment usually pays off. Just like we are intentional about setting our alarms to work out, I have to be intentional with making sure to greet my wife with a "Good morning," checking in during the day to see how she is doing, and not going to sleep without saying "Good night."

Greetings in the morning are important to me because it starts the day off the right way. A warm greeting may not seem like much, but I leave the house after just greeting my spouse with a smile on my face, and I am better prepared to take on the day ahead. I check in throughout the day because I know how busy my schedule is and how overwhelming my day's activities can be. If I need encouragement every now and then throughout the day, I check in to make sure she is being encouraged. I literally follow **Luke 6:38 (NIV), "Give, and it will be given to you. A good measure, pressed down, shaken together and running over, will be poured into your lap. For with the measure you use, it will be measured to you."**

If you need encouragement, are you encouraging others? If you need prayer, are you praying for others? Sometimes I call asking her to pray for me in a situation that just happened. We can limit our building with God and our spouses simply by not praying for them throughout the day. How powerful is it to know that someone is

calling to God on your behalf to meet every one of your car rides, cir-
cumstances, conversations, highs, interviews, lows, meetings, needs,
situations, you name it? To know someone is always interceding for
you is powerful! The check-in throughout the day is important and
should be intentional. You are not calling to argue or because you
need something; you are simply calling to check in and occasionally
let them know you are thinking about them. Finally, I check in at
night before going to sleep to ensure she survived the day. Her sur-
vival is important to me!

Surviving fiery days

First Corinthians 3:13–15 (NIV) tells us:

> *Their work will be shown for what it is, because
> the Day will bring it to light. It will be revealed
> with fire, and the fire will test the quality of
> each person's work. If what has been built sur-
> vives, the builder will receive a reward. If it is
> burned up, the builder will suffer loss but yet
> will be saved—even though only as one escap-
> ing through the flames.*

In summary, this verse lets you know that your works will be
tried by fire every day. Fire was a process used to purify metals and
stones and remove impurities that had attached themselves over time.
Similarly, there are things daily that attach themselves to how we
think, how we interact with our spouse, and what drives our moods.
Has stubbornness attached itself to you over the years? Has doubt
in your spouse attached itself to you over the years? When was the
last time you asked God to purge anything from your heart that
shouldn't be there?

*Psalm 51:10–12 (NIV) says, "Create in me a pure heart, O
God, and renew a steadfast spirit in me. Do not cast me from your
presence or take your Holy Spirit from me. Restore to me the joy*

of your salvation and grant me a willing spirit to sustain me." In these verses, we find David the giant slayer asking God to do what he could not do for himself in his heart and life. To have the strength and faith to kill Goliath in one chapter and then beg and plead for God to give him a clean heart in another chapter. I have found the strength to defeat so many things in life but struggle with communicating with my spouse or children. I need God's Holy Spirit to empower me to do things I can't do on my own, like loving my spouse unconditionally.

The second part of 1 Corinthians 3:15 is interesting. If your work is built to survive the fire or test of life at the end of the day, you will receive a reward. If not, you will suffer loss. But because of God's infinite mercy and grace, you will be saved. Have you ever intended to start a day off the right way and when your spouse says or does one thing opposite of what you were expecting, you default right back to stubborn behavior? It may just be me, but I have certainly burned my share of good-intentioned work for the day.

I realized my expectations of my spouse are very high while my expectations of others are lower. My spouse should have known not to do or to do something in my eyes. By now, *they should surely know I do or don't like things done a certain way,* but that is not always the case. I have been married for fifteen years, and I still am learning new things about my wife because she is always changing and growing. We must realize that every day since the day we first connected, we have changed in some way.

According to this scripture, each day has brought a different fire/test for us to navigate and experience. Sometimes we pass the test, and sometimes we take a loss. Don't be afraid to go through the fire or test of the day. If you seek God's help daily to be better, love better, and work better, over time, God will honor your efforts and slowly change your heart even when you get burned some days.

I can remember my wife and me arguing so intensely one time that we did not speak to each other for days. Not speaking to my spouse was a setback toward growth for the day. This was a loss for both of us. We allowed several days to go by that could have been adding rewards of greater love and victories of stronger communication in our marriage. It is a loss whenever we end our day with envy, impatience, jealousy, being mean, negativity, being short-tempered, and stubbornness to name a few. You and your spouse should be in your marriage with the goal of winning as much as possible.

> Victory in marriage requires individual sacrifice.

Passing the test each day is not easy. In college, you may have had a professor that would surprise the class with an unexpected test to see what you know. I didn't appreciate these kinds of surprises, but they taught me to always be ready. What if the professor told you at the beginning of the semester that he would give you a test every day? Would that change your intentionality for studying and preparing each day? God is saying to us individually and in our marriages that we will have a test every day, so how will we prepare?

Ending each day

When possible, I try to end the day with my spouse on a positive note. ***Ephesians 4:26 (NLT) states, "And don't sin by letting anger control you. Don't let the sun go down while you are still angry."*** It was easy when we first got married to remain in my feelings because that is what I was used to doing. If I got mad at someone, I would just leave. I could then sit in those feelings. Those feelings were comfortable. However, it was uncomfortable for me to admit to wrongdoing. We all have moments where convincing someone that you are right is more important than actually being right. There are countless arguments within my marriage that could have been avoided if I *actively* listened instead of just trying to be heard. Or I could have just apologized, even if I did not start it. Forgiveness is one of the most powerful things in our relationships.

One of my favorite accounts in the Bible is when the woman, who was a sinner, knew Jesus was present at a Pharisee's house. She came and poured expensive perfume on Jesus's head and washed his feet with her tears and hair. Everyone judged her and criticized her for being wasteful and irresponsible with her resources, but I love what Jesus said. *Luke 7:44–47 (NIV) tells us:*

> *Then He turned to the woman and said to Simon, "Do you see this woman? I entered your house; you gave Me no water for My feet, but she has washed My feet with her tears and wiped them with the hair of her head. You gave Me no kiss, but this woman has not ceased to kiss My feet since the time I came in. You did not anoint My head with oil, but this woman has anointed My feet with fragrant oil. Therefore I say to you, her sins, which are many, are forgiven, for she loved much. But to whom little is forgiven, the same loves little.*

The imagery alone moves my heart, but this scripture should resonate with you if you have ever needed forgiveness or extended forgiveness to others. No one is perfect, and forgiveness will be needed daily on this journey with your spouse. According to verse 47, if you want to love more, forgive more.

First Corinthians 13:11 (NIV) says, "When I was a child, I talked like a child, I thought like a child, I reasoned like a child. When I became a man, I put the ways of childhood behind me." You must also be careful that negative interactions between you and your spouse do not become comfortable. Human beings seek comfort in life. The more comfortable you become in negative communication, the harder it will be to see what's wrong with that type of communication. It will become normal for you.

Ephesians 4:26–27 (KJV) states, "Be ye angry, and sin not: let not the sun go down upon your wrath: Neither give place to the devil." The Bible is clear not to let anger rest with you overnight and not to give any place to the devil. I've learned that the longer we allow our feelings to take over, our comfort with negative feelings becomes greater. When you're not communicating well and not on the same page, you are acting more like two individuals instead of one flesh. It does not matter who's right or wrong. It's about learning how to get on the same page, aligned as one, quickly.

Before the end of the night, regardless of what happened in the day, if possible, I try to resolve actions, feelings, negative emotions, or thoughts, so I don't carry the past into the next day. I honestly am not always successful, but the effort is there to build my forgiveness and connection with Anjala daily. I'm developing a habit of consistently building communication and seeking to enjoy every moment of every day with my spouse.

In an interesting comparison, I am discovering that my relationship with God is likened to my relationship with my wife. ***Ephesians 5:25 (KJV) tells us, "Husbands, love your wives, even as Christ also loved the church, and gave himself for it."*** To strengthen our relationship, I must be intentional about speaking to God in the morning, throughout the day, and at night. I am constantly thinking about God throughout the day and looking forward to helping him however I can. Here are some examples:

1. I try to learn more about him daily to learn his likes and dislikes.
2. I honor him in my actions regardless of where I am or who I am with.
3. I sometimes go out of my comfort zone to do things that I wouldn't ordinarily do just to please him.

If I think about it, it sounds like my relationship with my wife. I am not saying that I worship my wife, or she is my God, but can you see the similarities in what it takes to build an intimate relationship? A relationship that is not fake or on the surface but is deep, growing, and strengthening daily. I can understand why Jesus, when asked by his disciples how to pray, said, "Give me this day my daily bread." Yesterday is gone, and tomorrow is not promised, so seize each day with the expectation that I will grow closer to my spouse come what may.

Simple prayer: Father, every day we experience is a new day with new mercies. You created us to have faith in you to rejoice and be glad every day, understanding the day is not promised. You are faithful. Help us to remain faithful to you and our marital relationships. Give us a heart after you to love better each day. In Jesus's name, amen!

CHAPTER 3

Every Week I'm Married

Three things you shouldn't lose this week;
your faith, your courage, and your smile.

—*Author unknown*

I love surprises (part 1)

Have you ever had a moment in life that pivoted how you viewed something forever? This summarizes our seventh year of marriage. It was a defining moment for me. I surprised my wife with a one-week trip to the Virgin Islands for our seventh year of marriage. I packed her bags, which was not easy, and coordinated with her job to request the time off. I also arranged for some trusted family members to watch our kids. The last step was finding a creative way to get her to the airport.

On the day of the trip, we got dressed for work like normal, and since we rode together, I didn't need to come up with a reason to be together that morning. We stopped by my job first, and instead of being dropped off, I picked something up from a coworker, then got back in the car and told her we were on our way to the airport. She was confused and shocked. She wanted to know where we were going, who was watching the kids, and who would fill in for her at work. I told her I had communicated with her supervisor and our family, and after the initial shock and a few confirmation phone calls, we got on a plane and made it to the Virgin Islands for one week of fun in the sun.

The trip was beautiful. We swam for hours in clear ocean water and enjoyed horseback riding on the beach. We went snorkeling for hours and committed to eating at a new place every day. We had tons of laughs and adventures while enjoying the beautiful sunshine. It was an amazing trip on so many levels, but it was also eye-opening for me. I found a marriage self-assessment questionnaire online, and we filled it out together. One of the questions asked, on a scale of 1 to 10, how would you rate your marriage? You could not have told me that we were not at a good place in our marriage. We made it to the seventh-year mark, and although we were not the standard for marriage, in my mind, we were doing okay. I learned never to assume I know what my spouse is thinking or feeling in the Virgin Islands. We can paint pictures of the perfect marriage and perfect communication, finances, security, sex, stability, and well-being. Unless you are truly listening to your spouse or simply asking questions, you will walk around with rose-tinted glasses slightly coloring your version of a stable marriage.

Anjala's response to the question was shockingly lower than I assumed. I honestly started crying when she expressed how she felt, and I actively listened to her heart. The week was supposed to be a week of fun and not my world being turned upside down. In hindsight, I am grateful for that moment, as it was a pivotal point that helped me learn to simply ask questions.

The importance of having something to look forward to

This is a busy time in our marriage. The kids have activities all the time, church and work are pulling, and this season seems crazier than ever. Balancing marriage, family, work, church, extracurricular activities, working out, and just being responsible can be overwhelming. It's as if we need a vacation and then another vacation right after to recover from the vacation we went on. Knowing that we have a trip planned helps us get through the day-to-day stuff. It gives us hope that relaxation and decompressing are on the way. Hope can be a lifesaver, especially when life weighs you down and your patience runs thin. Hope reminds me of the movie scenes where the character is about to die in the desert from dehydration, but right before passing out, they see a green oasis with water. That's what a vacation can be. In the midst of running out of energy, gas, patience, and steam, it can provide a lifeline. Reminding yourself that rest is on the way can give you that extra push/strength needed to continue.

My wife and I try, at a minimum, to have a weeklong vacation with our family every year. I characterize these weeklong vacations as having something to look forward to. These moments help me get through the busy times, knowing that a trip is planned and on the way soon.

If possible, I recommend longer, but I understand everyone's schedule and flexibility are different. The weeklong vacation gives you an opportunity to decompress from the world and your schedules, then spend time together building, growing, and loving each other. Again, if possible, I strongly encourage taking at least a week off. In a week, the first couple of days are usually spent recovering from preparing to take off. The next couple of days are enjoyable. The last couple is usually focused on shifting back into reality. If you are not able to take a week, try to take half of the week or an extended weekend. If you are not able to take two or three days, there are times when my spouse and I will take a personal day and will do nothing but be together. It is not about how much money you spend or how elaborate the trip is; it's more about the thoughtfulness and intentionality that goes into the time you spend.

Now that our children are older and more independent, we feel comfortable trusting them to be responsible, allowing us the latitude to do more things. We recently started a date night every week. My children know that every Wednesday night is time for my wife and me to go *out* or date *in*. They figure out their dinner and anything else while we spend time together. Being intentional about spending time with your spouse is important and key to a healthy marriage. I don't want the time we have been married to focus solely on building the kids and neglecting our marriage. It also gives us something to hope for throughout each week. Our date night should not seem like a religious activity that, if missed, we would be condemned. It is something meant to be part of strengthening our marriage. You can't expect to get physically stronger if you don't exercise, and you can't expect your marriage to strengthen if you are not building time together.

Again, the key is hope. If you have something to hope for in your marriage, it helps you maintain throughout the week. I love the scripture **Romans 4:18 (NIV), "Against all hope, Abraham in hope believed and so became the father of many nations, just as it had been said to him, 'so shall your offspring be.'"** At the age of ninety-nine, Abraham believed in God for a son. Based on his current situation, there was seemingly no hope that God could do it. Having faith in the hope that everything will work out has saved my marriage more times than I am willing to admit. I get in my feelings and can be stubborn, but I never lose *hope* in our marriage or us working the situation out. I have learned to take responsibility when I am at fault. Sometimes, however, it is my wife who is at fault. When this happens, I ask God to help me to communicate it in a way that builds her up instead of tearing her down or using it as a weapon to make me feel better. We are in this together, and *sharpening* each other must always be the goal.

Live for the day, build for each week

Our purpose for marriage is to show others God's light and power through us becoming one. That is not easy to do in general, let alone focus only on shining individually. In our house, we have several individual lights on one light fixture. Out of six lightbulbs, four may be out, and two are working. Because the two still provide light when we turn on the switch, we don't prioritize changing the other four because we have light. Does this sound familiar? Trust me, I get it. This is the mentality we can take into our marriages. We are still shining with love and finances, although the lights of intimacy, communication, spending time together, and hope have gone out. Your marriage is still together, but it is not shining the way God intended it. Not addressing areas where you are struggling in your marriage can put a strain on stronger areas, causing you to overcompensate, just like the light fixture. Now, if you are reading this and this is you, pause reading and go change your light bulbs.

Seriously, we can take on too much in a day and not realize it. *Matthew 6:34 (NIV) says, "Therefore do not worry about tomorrow, for tomorrow will worry about itself. Each day has enough trouble of its own."* Enough is going on right now in your life where you can easily worry and stress about tomorrow. Honestly, tomorrow is not promised to us. This book was written during a time in world history when a global pandemic, earthquakes, tropical storms, social and political struggles, family dysfunction, and divorces are rising. Life is precious and cannot be taken for granted. Live for this day, and don't worry about tomorrow. Instead, build for tomorrow. Building for tomorrow involves planning instead of panicking, working instead of worrying, developing instead of destroying, and living instead of losing what God has for you.

Are you allowing worry and the cares of this world to impact building with your spouse for the week? *Habakkuk 2:2–3 (ESV) states, "And the Lord answered me: Write the vision; make it plain on tablets, so he may run who reads it. For still the vision awaits its appointed time; it hastens to the end, it will not lie. If it seems slow, wait for it; it will surely come; it will not delay."* Each week, hold each other accountable and ask yourselves, "Are we fulfilling what God wanted us to this week?" We are imperfect and need to reference a perfect source. If we ask each other according to our own standards, we will always aim lower than what God has for us. Again, 1 Corinthians 13 should be your standard of love.

Worry affects our thoughts, our thoughts affect our work, and our work affects our faith. *James 2:20 (NLT) tells us, "How foolish! Can't you see that faith without good deeds is useless?"*

Faith that God can turn your marriage around is required but investing the work each day and planning to be successful each week helps keep that faith alive. Marriage requires daily work and weekly building! Be intentional about living for today. Don't let this moment continue to be wasted or pass you by. Apologize if you need to. Go out on a date. Flirt with your spouse. Make them something special. Post something sweet about them on social media. Send them an unexpected gift (within reason, nothing that would cause more strain). Build for the week. Review the budget together. Invest in a financial planner. Write down your collective goals for the next one, three, five, or even ten years. Whatever it is, don't be complacent with two out of six lightbulbs working in your marriage. Invest in writing the vision and put in the work to shine as bright as you can for God.

The importance of praying weekly and together in marriage

For years, my wife and I led a weekly prayer call at our church. If I am honest, I did not always feel like praying when we first began. In the beginning, it felt like a burden. It was like when you first started exercising after not doing it for so long. My drive and focus were not having it. Boy, has that changed! I've prayed so much now; interceding with my wife for each other and others is one of the best parts of my week. I truly believe that our communication and genuineness toward each other is largely due to God honoring us after praying together every week. Prayer helps build your relationship with God, but prayer with your spouse builds God's strength, resilience, and resolve in your marriage. Prayer in your marriage is extremely important. Prayer has bound our marriage together spiritually, mentally, emotionally, and even physically. But like working out, if you don't keep up with it, the lack of prayer could weaken a marriage.

One fall morning, I woke up like usual and started my day. After getting dressed and freshening up, I headed out the door, and to my surprise, did not see my wife's car in the driveway. I called my wife and asked her if she had moved the car. With a confused response, she said no. I said, "I think somebody stole our car." We were both in disbelief. This does not happen to *us*. Our first response was honestly panic. We didn't know who, what, when, where, or how, but it happened to *us*. I will never forget our response after the initial reaction. It's like a sudden peace came over both of us. We were literally in a place where our car was stolen, and Anjala and I both were resolved that if God allowed it to happen, he must have something better in store!

I recently heard someone quote Psalm 84:11 in a way I never heard before. *Psalm 84:11 says, "For the Lord God is a sun and shield; the Lord bestows favor and honor; no good thing does he withhold from those whose walk is blameless."* Paraphrasing, they said, since God will not withhold any good thing from you, even on bad days, you are winning. That to me is the power and benefit of prayer! Prayer is not always for the *moment*, but it helps to prepare you for the moments in life. I have cried and poured out my heart to God in private and in prayer, so when our moment came, God replaced worry and concern with his peace.

Isaiah 26:3 (KJV) states, "Thou wilt keep him in perfect peace, whose mind is stayed on thee: because he trusteth in thee." God ultimately returned our car back to us with minimal damage, but more than praising God for the car returned, I praised him for the peace provided during an unexpected storm.

> Prayer is a guard for the unexpected things in life.

If you knew what was going to happen and when it would happen, you would prepare; but since we don't know what tomorrow holds, the best thing is to stay in constant communication with the One who does. God knows how to turn your marriage, relationships, and present situations around from being on the brink of divorce to loving each other more than ever. *Psalm 46:1 (KJV) tells us, "God is our refuge and strength, a very present help in trouble."* Prayer in my marriage doesn't always stop things from happening, but it places me in constant contact with God the Father. I can call on him, and he immediately comes to my rescue. That's the type of relationship I am seeking to have with God.

Fifty-two weeks go by before you know it

God created everything in six days, and on the seventh day, he rested from all creation. One day was devoted to intentionally stopping the week's grind and resting. Do you make time in your marriage to rest individually and with your husband or wife? This time is often overlooked and undervalued. I get it. I struggled in this area too. When my family and I relocated from Michigan to Georgia for my job, Anjala was not working. She stayed with the kids and took a break from work to help us get settled in Georgia. During this season, I worked a lot of hours throughout the week, and I came home late at night after leaving early every morning.

One day, I asked my wife if there was anything I could do to help around the house, and she said, "The kids and I could see you more." Something about that really struck me to the core. By working hard to provide for my family, I thought I was being a great father and husband, but from my wife's perspective, she just wanted more time with me. It is not that she did not appreciate my efforts, I was just too busy, and as a result, was missing out on my family.

I recently went into a local auto parts store and to my pleasant surprise, learned that a friend managed the store. I was really excited to see him, and we exchanged contact information and spoke about connecting soon to catch up and talk about achieving plans for early retirement. Fast forward a couple of months, I go by the store and ask for him. One of the clerks asked me whom I was talking about. I questioned if I had his name correct since we recently connected after not seeing each other for some time. I went into my phone to a text message we shared a month ago, and I indeed had his name correct. I stated his name to the clerk again in greater confidence only to learn that the reason the clerk was questioning me was that my friend died in a car accident a month earlier, and they were shocked that I was asking for him. This exchange really shook me up, and I still think about the importance of tomorrow not being promised.

Time goes by so fast. If you are not careful, you can blink and miss it. I recently was thinking about the impact the global pandemic has had on relationships. Has it brought your family closer together or driven you further apart? Does it have you wishing and hoping for everything to open back up so you can escape your family? Have you dreaded working from home with your spouse and children on their virtual calls? Only you know for certain, but I will tell you, you will never get this time back ever again.

My twin children are ten, and my oldest is twelve years old. I cannot relive or get back the time with my children at their current ages. Similarly, I cannot redo a conversation or moment spent with my wife. This isn't the movies where you can go back in time. Good, bad, right, or wrong, the point is, cherish your time. There are literally fifty-two weeks in a year. That may seem like a lot of time, but it goes by so fast. Enjoy the day and build on each week.

Simple prayer: Father, every week is a week you have made, and we acknowledge and are grateful. Help us to be creative in how we love and strengthen our relationships. You are the ultimate Creator, and let us not undervalue the importance of you in our lives. Let our hunger and thirst for you never be quenched, and allow us to experience your love each week of our marriage and lives. In Jesus's name, amen!

CHAPTER 4

Every Month I'm Married

*Cheers to a new month and another
chance for us to get it right.*

—*Oprah Winfrey*

December is our month. Do you have a month that's yours?

Our family loves the month of December. My wife loves decorating and transforming the house into a Christmas catalog. By December first, Anjala has fully decorated the house with four to five Christmas trees and is usually done with at least half the Christmas shopping. We usually have Christmas lights on the outdoor bushes, trees, and lining our garage. Rudolf and Frosty are there to keep the wreath on our door company. If you walk in, you may smell winter pine or some sort of sweet cookie candle that has been prepared to greet every house guest. Although we only have three children, Anjala insists that we keep at least ten stockings in case someone with a child stops by, and she feels the need to make them feel special. In December, we generally are prepared for any holiday surprises.

In a similar fashion, we use December as our month to prepare for the following year. But it is also an intentional time of reflection. Taking time to reflect on the year is important. Reflection is powerful. Have you developed and reflected on the goals you were hoping to accomplish this year? Oftentimes, couples may reflect on finances, careers, and even goals centered around their children. But do you take time to reflect on your progress toward perfecting your love according to 1 Corinthians 13:4–8? Calibrate and adjust before heading into the new year with the same bad habits and unhealthy practices. As warm and fuzzy as December makes us, we should be prepared to have some uncomfortable conversations and adjustments as well.

Am I comfortable with the uncomfortable?

> *Comfort in the wrong context, can be damaging to your marriage. Uncomfortable conversations can be difficult but are required. (Marcus Huff)*

When I think of comfort, I think of warmth, relaxation, a hot beverage, and a great movie. I picture myself on the couch, in front of a fire, wearing my favorite pair of pajamas that I have had for at least five years. You know, the ones with the hole that your wife wants you to get rid of? That's comfort. Or maybe you have a man cave that has all of your favorite items—TV, fridge, and a wonderful recliner. During the global pandemic of 2020, everyone was forced to stay indoors which may have redefined your definition of comfort. Some of us were working, helping our children attend school, and even vacationing in our home. I thank God I can honestly say I enjoyed the time with my wife and family, but I do know that is not everyone's testimony.

Being at home so much allowed my wife the opportunity to remind me of everything she wanted redone in the home. We renovated our bathroom, redecorated three bedrooms, and redesigned our living room. When we realized it would be awhile before we would vacation again, we hired a contractor to redo our backyard, so we could enjoy more time together in an outdoor space just for us. It was a nice change of environment and created a new comfortable place for our family to enjoy and settle in. This type of comfort can be refreshing and needed in our marriages, but another comfort can produce the opposite effects.

One of the things we struggled with in the early years of marriage was allowing too much time to pass with unresolved issues. As I mentioned earlier, both of us wrestle with stubbornness, and we would be completely comfortable and content with allowing months to pass without directly addressing issues and concerns that arose. The danger with that amount of time passing is the comfort that comes with time. The longer you allow problems to linger and go unresolved, the more comfortable you get in that space. Finding comfort in stubbornness, arrogance, condescension, pride, doubt, fear, worry, and mistrust is not healthy for you or your marriage. If we are being honest, how often do we allow things to go unresolved? Are you becoming comfortable with avoiding conflict and creating distance? Are you comfortable diving deeper into social media instead of into the work required to resolve the tension between you and your wife or husband? These are a few habits that damage a healthy marriage environment.

God recently showed me a scripture about stubbornness that shook up my life. In the Bible, Samuel rebukes King Saul, the first king of Israel, for disobeying God. ***First Samuel 15:23a (NLT) says, "Rebellion is as sinful as witchcraft, and stubbornness as bad as worshipping idols."*** My stubbornness is as bad as worshipping idols? Wait. What? So in God's eyes, my stubbornness is the equivalent of making something else my god instead of God? It's the equivalent of giving praise and worship and time and energy to the god of stubbornness than the God of the universe? I was truly convicted. I may be taking this to the extreme, but the word of God can convict you in a way that nothing else can.

Recently, I was on a podcast and asked about problem-solving in marriage. I stated, "If problem-solving is the destination, the car you want to be in is *communication*." Communication is a vehicle you cannot afford to go cheap on. Healthy communication is communicating through the uncomfortable things in your marriage. I will explain this more in a moment, but it's important to avoid habits that cause you to be fearful of tackling tough topics in your marriage. This is not a charge for men to be arrogant or prematurely force a conversation because they want to discuss it *right now*. This used to mess me up all the time in the early years of our marriage. I would force a conversation with my wife to the point of an emotional and mental attack or even verbal abuse, and my wife simply did not want to talk at that time. We were missing each other communication wise. I used to think she was trying to be in control when we talked or was even avoiding discussions. If you know my wife, she does not have the personality of someone who easily backs down from a conflict. It wasn't until later that I realized she simply wanted a moment to calm down before speaking. She was aware of her emotions and didn't want to say anything out of anger. She was doing our marriage and me a favor!

Healthy communication

> *Healthy communication is knowing how to address the uncomfortable things in your marriage. (Marcus Huff)*

The first thing that helped me have healthier communication in my marriage was staying prayerful! If *communication* is an area you struggle in, talk to God first before talking to your spouse. Ask God and the Holy Spirit to be present in your conversation. I don't always have the right words, but God does. There may be someone reading this and saying, "I have tried that before, and it doesn't work." Keep talking to God because it is not falling on deaf ears. God is not deaf.

If praying alone is not working, try fasting. In Matthew 17, a father comes to Jesus's disciples, asking them to deliver his son from a demon that is causing him to hurt himself. The disciples could not deliver him, and then Jesus arrives on the scene. The father explains what happened, and Jesus immediately rebukes the demon and delivers the son. Later, the disciples ask Jesus why they couldn't deliver the son from the demon, and Jesus says because of their lack of faith. But he also states some things only come out through both *prayer and fasting*. Try both prayer and fasting if one is not effective.

The second thing that has helped me have healthier communication is *staying calm*. I heard a marriage counselor once say, "When your emotions go up, intelligence goes down." I don't know the science behind this, but it always speaks to my heart. When I get angry, my heart rate goes all the way up, and I get defensive. I just start talking with the goal of shutting down anyone or anything trying to offend me. If you are like me, you must calm down. Take a moment and breathe. Walk away until you can reengage respectfully. Extend each other the grace and space to calm down; it will significantly help your communication.

The third thing is to try to hear the heart behind what your spouse is saying, even when it is not communicated in the best way. You may be hearing your spouse say something offensive but if you know they are coming from a loving place, communicate the disconnect to them. "I am hearing you say this to me. Can you please clarify what you are trying to say so that I am not taking your words out of context?"

Early in our marriage, we were still getting to know each other, but my expectations for Anjala were so high that I could not even live up to them. I expected her to know how I felt and understand my reaction in each situation. That is just not realistic. I barely know how I am going to react to different situations, yet I was expecting my spouse to teach a masterclass on me? This was just unfair. Again, extending grace in marriage is required. We all have moments where we mean one thing and say another. Work toward getting clarity on each other's hearts and pray to God for grace to give you the right words to say.

The fourth thing is to move beyond a self-centered perspective. When I first got married, I didn't realize it wasn't all about me, myself, and I. I struggled with getting past my own perspective and opinion. I still have to remind myself that although I am in the marriage, my marriage cannot revolve around me. *Galatians 6:3 (KJV) says, "For if a man think himself to be something, when he is nothing, he deceives himself."* When my perspective is the only perspective, I can live a deceiving life. That's why you should seek counsel from counselors, mentors, or accountability couples about marriage. Seeking advice from others is humbling because you don't know it all, and you are not always right. Humble yourself and be open to another perspective. Having to face the reality that the world does not revolve around you can be uncomfortable but looking past yourself is worth it for the sake of your marriage.

The last thing is don't be petty. People can be pompous, condescending, and sarcastic. These things don't lead to stronger communication or strengthening your marriage. Honestly, addressing these things can be uncomfortable and challenging. You naturally want to avoid, push back, defend, and be distant. Addressing historical habits and traits is absolutely necessary. Learn to incorporate good habits throughout your day-to-day life. Learn to be a better communicator at work and at church and with coworkers, strangers, and neighbors. This will help you be a better communicator with your spouse.

Unhealthy communication

> Unhealthy communication is not addressing the "comfortable" things. (Marcus Huff)

What was comfortable for me going into my marriage was stubbornness, unresolved issues, and emotional distance. If my wife didn't want to talk to me, I was content with not wanting to talk to her. The comfort of staying in this type of place is dangerous for your marriage. Knowing how to address things that may be naturally comfortable for you, but are not helpful for you, is important. In addition, lying or manipulation may be something you have leaned on in your life, and it is now comfortable for you to lie about small things. The comfort of lying will lead to unhealthy communication and an unhealthy marriage. Regardless of the negative habit, you should break habits that have been negatively comfortable in your past.

The Bible is full of uncomfortable conversations between God and man, like in Genesis 3:8–19 when the serpent tricked the woman, and the woman convinced the man to disobey God, introducing sin into the world. The conversation God had with Adam and Eve was uncomfortable and probably the first uncomfortable conversation ever.

The conversation between Peter and Paul in Galatians 2:11–14 was uncomfortable. Peter would eat with the Gentiles, but when his Jewish friends came around, he was afraid of what the Jews would say and distanced himself from the Gentiles. Paul ended up confronting Peter publicly in front of everyone. I am sure that was an uncomfortable conversation, but it needed to happen because it was starting to impact others. I want to pause here because allowing comfortable negative habits to continue doesn't just impact you, but these negative habits impact your purpose, marriage, family, community, and world.

> When you all are not the best version
> of the *oneness* God created you to be,
> it impacts those connected to you.

I want to emphasize that addressing comfortable things is critical in your marriage. A trend I see when providing marriage counseling is the comfort of not speaking to each other for days, weeks, and even months on end after an intense disagreement or argument. The comfort of acting like you don't care what happens to your spouse after an intense exchange is an unhealthy communication habit. My dad used to say the opposite of love is not hate but indifference. To stop caring is arguably the opposite of love. Whether you agree or not, you don't want to develop habits that distance you and your spouse from healthy communication but rather strengthen unconditional love in your marriage. The Bible declares that you and your spouse are one. So, in essence, to say that you don't care about what they are doing or where they are is saying you don't care about yourself. Not caring may or may not be the opposite of love, but it is certainly not a comfortable place you want to be in your marriage.

A common thread in all these instances mentioned in the Bible passages and often in our lives is a selfish perspective taken by the individual or individuals in each account. Eve saw that it could be *good for her* to eat regardless of what God said. So she ate. Peter wanted to *fit in* more than he wanted to do what was right. It sounds crazy to read someone else doing it, but if I am honest, I do it all the time. I only focus on my perspective and get mad at God and others if they do not agree or fall in line with my way of doing things. Selfishness is a destroyer of relationships and brings justification to those who are self-centered. I needed to grow up for the sake of my marriage and purpose. I speak to encourage anyone else that needs to do the same. ***First Corinthians 13:11 (NLT) tells us, "When I was a child, I spoke and thought and reasoned as a child. But when I grew up, I put away childish things."***

We are either building together or apart

Since 2020, the past few years have increased online and virtual communication given the global pandemic. Due to virtual technology, families, friends, school, and even business interactions have taken on a new meaning. It has been helpful, but it has also presented challenges. It's so easy to get distracted and to multitask when you are hiding behind a screen. Likewise, if my wife and I are not careful, we can spend hours in the same room but be distant as she navigates online, and I do the same. It's interesting to think you can be together and still be so far away from each other.

There are twelve months in a year, and with each passing month, you are either building closer together or apart. Time waits for no one, and you must be intentional about the time you invest in each other. I am not the same person my wife married fifteen years ago. I dress differently, think differently, and see things differently than when we first got married. Growing and maturing as individuals will happen. Growth is a part of life. As you grow, a key question is: are you growing together or growing apart?

I believe we all need someone to talk especially when times are challenging. Let that someone be your spouse. Be intentional about communicating with your spouse about your day. It can be the smallest detail or the biggest event. The more you learn how to share with each other, the stronger your marriage will become. It may not always be easy to listen. We sometimes get distracted by everything else going on or even by our desire to be doing something else, but take the time to build listening muscles. Your spouse will communicate, one way or another, their heart's passions, ambitions, dreams, goals, and desires, and you don't want to miss it. Poor listening will discourage your spouse from communicating with you. Trust me, if your spouse is not telling you their heart, they are telling it to someone else.

Get into a habit of going on a date at least monthly. Take time out each month to do something special for your spouse. Show them how much you appreciate them at least twelve times a year. I often think about all the things my wife does for our family and me, and I am in awe. She is an amazing woman! She works, keeps everyone in the house in line, co-labors in ministry, and is a friend to the friendless and a mother to the motherless. *I am somewhat kidding*, but I appreciate her and enjoy hanging out with her. If we can't find twelve times throughout the year to have personal and intentional time growing in our marriage, we need to do better.

Habits are key

Every month in 2021, our family committed the first week of the month to God. We spent the week having Bible study; fasting from things that are typically distractions like playing on laptops, video games, or social media; and enjoying each other's company by playing games or simply hanging out together. Our children led Bible studies throughout the week, each taking a day to speak on a passage out of the Bible or from a Bible plan. It helped to bring us all together and strengthen our family's spiritual bond and connections.

Doing things repeatedly can cause them to become a part of your routine. This is what I think about when I think of habits. Each month, choose a good habit to create within your marriage.

A month affords you approximately thirty days to pick up good habits and get rid of bad ones. The more positive things you feed yourself, the more positive things you can pull from when needed. The more negative things you feed yourself, the more negative things you have to pull from. Put down the phone for a least one week throughout the month. Go on a walk or exercise. Go out on a date. Send your wife or husband flowers or do something unexpected they will enjoy. Husbands, clean up the house, and have the children fed and in bed early. Put important dates on your calendar, so you are intentional about remembering. Wives, take your husband to a game or a movie he really wants to see. Either one of you can write poems or love letters, plan a trip, buy your spouse's favorite sweets, or take them to their favorite restaurant. The list goes on and on. But the point is if you can make time for work, family, church, friends, social media, and life, make time to develop good habits by building a relationship with your spouse.

On the other side, be aware of negative habits like not speaking to each other or shutting down when you get angry. Don't fall into the trap of telling others how you feel instead of telling your spouse or always putting your children first before your spouse. Don't be condescending or sarcastic. Be careful not to value your own thoughts above your spouse's. Don't build the habits of not listening, being easily angered, quick to speak, slow to hear, and not working toward making any of the love standards identified in 1 Corinthians 13:4–7 your standard. A month doesn't seem like a lot of time, but as mentioned earlier in this chapter, you can grow closer together or further apart with each passing day. Which one are you shifting toward?

I encourage you not to live life selfishly but develop positive habits, be willing to be uncomfortable in your communication, and identify the month in the year that will be your month even if it doesn't appear that positive communication, praying for your spouse, and spending time with your family are helping you all stay together. Taking time to become a better person is not easy. Thinking of others more than yourself is not easy. Some are still single because they subconsciously and consciously get anxiety about having to consider others in their daily routines. Trust me. Marriage, raising a family, helping others, being selfless, choosing good habits over wrong ones, treating your neighbor right—all these things are not easy, but they are worth it. There are twelve months in a year, and be intentional about how you spend each one.

All about me, myself, and I

The Enemy of time is Selfishness. (Marcus Huff)

When I do things with selfish motives, they rarely afford long-term satisfaction. It may give me a temporary feeling or sense of accomplishment, but in the end, I feel void of something that only comes from doing things for others. My wife recently showed me a video of someone she follows on social media. It is a guy that works at a convenience store, and he strategically places expensive items in places in the store for people to randomly find them. If people who find them come back and are honest about what they found, he gives them what they found or often blesses them even more than before. The thing I appreciate about the videos is the people's sincere reaction to someone doing something for them they did not expect. The rush of emotion and appreciation that comes over them can be felt and is inspiring enough to push me to do and be better.

There are other videos on social media where people solely focus on themselves. Both get attention, but which one do you aspire to? Do you desire to promote and do things that bring attention to you and your needs or the needs and lives of others?

Recognizing and acknowledging in my marriage that I am self-centered was difficult for me. It was hard for me to recognize and even more challenging to admit. Getting to this place has taken time and a lot of unnecessary conflicts for me to notice. Now that I am aware, I am more conscious of the behavior and the subtle ways it impacts my daily interaction with my wife. Being self-centered has not always led to a damaging conversation or moment in my marriage, but I am noticing it can create habits that are not healthy for our long-term journey. Recently it has shown up in my desire to want to be a better listener. I will ask about my wife's day and as she tells me, I will start off listening but then find myself bringing it back to my day. It is subtle, but she starts off talking about her day, and if I am not intentional about listening and being supportive, I will shift from her completely to about my day. This example may seem extreme but having a perspective focused solely on you can rear its head in subtle ways.

Psalm 51:10 (KJV) says, "Create in me a clean heart, O God; and renew a right spirit within me." I often pray this scripture to God to help combat my selfish ways. This scripture lets me know that my heart has the ability to get dirty. Dirt can come from things I watch and take in, conversations and thoughts I have, or even from good intentions. Have you ever planned a date for you and your spouse, but it was at a place you like, and they are your plus one? They have an attitude or may not be enjoying themselves as much as you, and you are irritated and justified in your irritation because you were doing something nice for them and they are being ungrateful. Maybe I am the only one who has done this before but not that I am calling my heart dirty because of this, but it reminds me of things that are covering up my heart that are causing me not to recognize the heart of my spouse or others. I don't want to live with a heart covered up, but I want God to create a clean heart in me so that I love purely and without taint.

The second part of the verse speaks about renewing the right spirit in me. I would boast that I have a good spirit overall, but when I am tired or hungry, my spirit's batteries go down, and if it is not renewed, I become the Hulk in all the wrong ways. That's why you need people in your life starting with God who will not always agree with your perspective but are willing to challenge you to be better. If you hang around a lot of like-minded people, you will all see the same and never challenge each other. But God's word challenges me all the time, and I additionally keep people in my life that are headed places I aspire to be.

If you think at any time in your marriage you have been or are currently selfish, my prayer would be that you recognize and acknowledge a need to change. The more time you allow to pass without addressing the subtlety of selfishness, the more embedded in your character it will become. When I was a kid, I used to say and hear often, "It's all about me, myself, and I." I unknowingly was teaching myself at a young age whom I cared about. This was childish, playful, and some may call innocent, but according to *1 Corinthians 13:11 (KJV), "When I was a child, I talked like a child. I thought like a child. I had the understanding of a child. When I became a man, I put the ways of childhood behind me."* We all have to grow up, and the hope is when you do, you no longer think and behave the same. Be determined each month this year to stretch your growth toward the goal of fulfilling God's purpose for your life and marriage.

Simple prayer: Father, each month presents an opportunity for growth, stretching, and to be closer to you. Help our intentionality each month to be focused on strengthening our marriage. Help us not get weary in doing well but stick to doing those things that are good, lovely, and helpful to our personal lives and the lives of our neighbors. In Jesus's name, amen!

CHAPTER 5

Every Year I'm Married

*What the new years brings to you will depend a
great deal on what you bring to the new year.*

—Vern McLellan

I love surprises (part 2)

For my wife's thirty-second birthday, I wanted to do something special. Through God's help, I pulled together $100 for every year she was born. We have three children, and I had each of the children bring in a stack of $100 bills until she received it all. It was a gift she often reminds me of and says she would be completely content to get this every birthday. It's important to create memories that are lasting and impactful. It doesn't have to be big, like $100 every year, but it should be thoughtful and personal. Taking the time to be creative and planning out a gift usually leaves a lasting impression. It lets my spouse know I'm thinking about them, and they are always on my mind. After fifteen years of marriage, I am still trying to win her heart over. Is there at least one thing you can reflect on in the year you did for your spouse that stands out and was special? If not, you can certainly accomplish one thing per year, right?

Reflect and reconnect

Every year, typically in the winter, Anjala and I take time to reflect on the year and plan for the future. We get away from kids, day-to-day work, and the busyness of life and have a goal-setting session to reflect on the years to come. Some years we can get a weekend away, and some years we simply go out to eat. The importance is the intentionality of the time invested with your spouse. Now watch this; according to ***Ecclesiastes 3:1 (KJV), "To every thing there is a season, and a time to every purpose under the heaven."*** Every season is different, and tradition should be removed by the leading of the Holy Spirit. At the end of 2021, we had a vision session with our family. We gathered around a table full of magazines and paper and wrote down and thought about our upcoming year. We developed the vision boards over music and fun and then prayed over the boards and God's plan for the upcoming year.

Jesus understood the importance of getting away from it all and just spending time with God. On several occasions, he intentionally took time away to pray and communicate with God. ***Luke 5:16 (NIV) says, "But Jesus often withdrew to the wilderness for prayer."*** When was the last time you intentionally got away from it all for just you and your spouse? You and your family? You and God? Setting aside time for prayer or reading your Bible? A few years ago, my wife and I read a book together that focused on goal setting. It asked us to write down our one-year, three-year, five-year, and ten-year goals. We completely approached the exercise differently, and I learned that's okay. I started setting goals at one year and worked my way to ten years, and Anjala looked at where she wanted to be in ten years and worked back to how to get there in one year. I liked her way better and redid my goals based on her approach. Whatever your approach, I recommend investing time to identify your collective goals and then go after them.

Although we don't look at our goals from that exercise every day of the year, we review them quarterly or certainly during our annual getaway. We reflect to see if we are tracking according to what we said and if not, we adjust based on the season we are in at the time.

Individual goals are not only a road map for you toward accomplishing your goals, but they help your spouse know what your vision is and allow them the opportunity to help and support you to get there. When you reflect, don't give place to the devil and use the time to add stress, blame, or cause arguments for things you didn't accomplish; that's not the point of the exercise. The point of the exercise is to reflect, grow, and align dreams, desires, and outcomes for your future. It's okay if your goals change. As you grow and build together, your goals will continue to evolve and develop.

Wait, when did we change?

My wife and I are pretty chill, and we tend to live a low-stress lifestyle (for us). This was epitomized on our wedding day. Our theme was *simply put*, and from the menu (catered by family), to the colors (black and white with red accents), and to the venue (church Anjala grew up in), our wedding day was low stress. I can remember thinking, *Okay, this is going well.* Where is the wedding-movie moment when something goes awry? But it never happened. Praise God!

Over the years, we have grown more, and we both are still pretty chill but in different ways than when we first got married. For example, when we first got married, my wife could not rest if the kitchen or bedroom was not clean. I mean clean, clean. Over time, three kids later, it relaxed a slight bit, and as of recent, cleaning has shifted to the kids doing most of the cleaning. As a parent wanting to raise responsible children, Anjala had to give up the desire to have everything cleaned as she liked it in the journey of teaching my kids the level of cleanliness she expects.

I was a loner. I didn't really hang out with others much, but now I enjoy company more often than I used to. Are we no longer the same people? Did we get transformed into someone else? Not at all. My wife is probably more loving now than she has ever been, but something changed in both of us over time. Change is not a bad thing and is a part of life. I have learned to appreciate the change that is gradual instead of hard-hitting.

EVERY YEAR I'M MARRIED

> I would rather wake up next to my spouse
> and appreciate how they have grown in
> grace over the years than look over and not
> recognize the person they have become.

I think about individuals in the Bible—men and women of God who were connected to strong influences but somehow ended up making different decisions. It makes me ask what happened and when did this person change? In 1 Samuel 25, it talks about a married couple. The husband's name is Nabal, and his wife's name is Abigail. Nabal was wealthy and from a place called Maon but was characterized as being churlish and evil in his business dealings while his wife was described by her beauty and someone of good understanding.

David, the giant slayer, was in the area and sent his men to Nabal to humbly request food since he had treated Nabal kindly, not taking anything from him or hurting his sheep. Nabal, in turn, responded to David very harshly. When David heard his response, he was furious and was going to kill everyone. But Abigail heard about what happened and intervened. She sent food to David and his men, which calmed David and his men down, and they left.

Later on, she comes home, and Nabal is partying. The next day, she told him what had happened. He heard about it and had a stroke and eventually died. David finds out and goes back to marry Abigail. Crazy story, I know, but Nabal and Abigail seemed like opposites. We don't know their backstories. I wonder if they both were always like that, or maybe Nabal was kind at one point, and the money and success changed him. Who knows?

The point is that I believe our experiences inform the decisions we make about situations over time. If you are not careful, you can find yourself a completely different person in a not-so-good way, shifting not only who you were but whom you would like to be. There have been countless times when I struggled with feelings of pride and stubbornness trying to wash over me to drown out my desire to want to get out of my feelings. There are even times I felt I was watching myself act in a way I didn't want to. I may be the only one, but I don't like becoming someone I am not proud of nor recognize. The truth is, you are constantly changing, growing, learning new things, and embracing new perspectives whether you realize it or not. Again, to have a mentality that you are not going to change, that this is who you are and who you were when they married you, is not helpful for your marriage.

My wife often talks about flowers and weeds. In order for flowers to grow, they need attention. They need sunlight and water. Some people talk to their plants to give them the oxygen they need. Others give them fertilizer and prune some branches that are not growing as good as others. We had some plants growing in our house, and not only did they require those things, but the environment in which they were placed was equally important. We had to move it in front of a window on the east side of the house. In summary, it took intentionality for the flowers or plants to grow and flourish. In contrast, weeds don't need much to survive. They flourish in inconvenient places and in almost any environment. You don't have to be intentional about helping them to grow; they just appear naturally. You don't have to invest time or talk to them if you let them be; they will find a way to appear.

This is a perfect analogy for positive and negative behavior. You don't have to work at being a negative person; it seems like we naturally gravitate toward negativity. Whether a negative environment, group of friends, social media feed, conversations, thinking, and actions, negativity finds ways to creep into our lives, hearts, and minds naturally. If you have ever tried to get weeds out, unless you get them at the root, time and opportunity are all that are required for them to reappear. To be positive and kind, it takes intentionality until it becomes a part of who you are.

Maybe your environment or people you hang around need to change. Maybe the things you feed yourself need to change. Maybe you need to prune or cut back some things or relationships. Weeds or negative habits seem to come naturally. Positive habits require work, but you have to be resolved that your marriage and the purpose for your marriage are worth it.

Don't let years past and negativity grow in you. Make up in your mind that you will and can change into the person God has called you to be and your spouse needs you to be. If you genuinely believe in the Bible and that the two of you are now one, don't be okay with treating yourself negatively. When I am disrespectful to my spouse, I am disrespectful to myself. When I talk about how she looks or where I believe she is falling short, I am talking about myself. When I am not willing to help her because I believe she made the mess or caused the problem, I am doing that to myself.

Negativity is like a weed that should be taken out from the root. Don't let feelings of resentment, jealousy, and even poor communication take root. *First Peter 5:7 (NLT) states, "Give all your worries and cares to God, for he cares about you."* Learn to give your worries to God. Let negative things you are holding on go and move on. Learn from your mistakes, and don't repeat them. Destruction and divorce are usually things that occur over time. *Galatians 5:9 says, "You should know that 'just a little yeast works its way through the whole batch of dough.'"* Just allowing a little bit of negativity over time can impact you deeply.

One scripture I often reflect on is *Ephesians 4:26–27 (NKJV), "Be angry, and do not sin: do not let the sun go down on your wrath, nor give place to the devil."* We all get angry, and it sometimes feels we are quicker to get angry with our spouse than with coworkers, friends, or even strangers. It's as if we have the highest expectations from our spouse and hold them to a standard higher than we hold ourselves. Our spouses will mess up, fall short, let us down, irritate us, and may even cause us to want to sin, but I have learned it is the devil trying to get a place in our marriage. The devil is constantly trying to break up the connection between you and your husband or wife. He will try to use your past, present, friends, family, children, God's Word—whatever he can to bring you to divorce or division.

Learn to resolve things this year, and don't ever give any place to the devil. Don't give him anger in your marriage. Your marriage is between you and your spouse. Publicizing your spouse's negative behavior on social media, speaking rudely or harshly to your spouse, or other things that will bring you apart are not helpful. Fight for your marriage like you would fight for yourself.

I put you first

Wherever your treasure is, there the desires of your heart will also be. (Matthew 6:21 NLT)

When my first child, Brooklynn, was born, she was premature and weighed a total of three pounds five ounces. Anjala did an amazing job during labor, and it overall was a great delivery. Brooklynn was born early on Sunday morning. Ironically, I was scheduled to speak at church that morning. My wife was very clear that she did not want me to leave the hospital that Sunday morning, but for whatever reason, I decided to go anyway.

Two years later, my wife is getting ready to deliver twins and they are born early Sunday morning. Because of what happened during Brooklynn's birth, my wife clearly stated she did not want me to leave, even if I was scheduled to preach that Sunday. Can you guess if wisdom prevailed this time around? No, I decided to speak, and that decision caused a rift in our marriage for some time. I thank God in heaven that my wife is a forgiving person! Love covers a multitude of sins indeed.

Now let me pause and address the thoughts that are flooding some of your minds. If God told you to go, then you should always be obedient to God's voice and put him first above your spouse, family, and anything else, always and without question. The question I have wrestled with in hindsight has been "Was God pulling me to go or self?" Now, when you say you put your spouse and family first, do your actions follow your words? You can be busy doing a lot of different things, things that may feel important to you, but if you are not communicating with your spouse, those busy things can be unproductive for your marriage.

This is how I felt in the early years of my marriage. I was busy doing different things I thought would benefit my marriage, but I was not investing in productive activities that helped strengthen my marriage. We can be busy with activities in our marriages but not listen or hear what our spouses really need. When we first moved to Georgia from Michigan, I was busy at work and invested a lot of hours at the job. Since my job had moved my family and me down, I felt I owed them that. Don't get me wrong; being responsible with your work is vital to your well-being, but it must be balanced. ***Proverbs 11:1 (KJV) tells us, "A false balance is an abomination to the Lord: but a just weight is his delight."*** In all my doing at work, I neglected to do at home.

It is just as easy to find yourself busy at church or serving in some capacity. When we first started attending our church in Georgia, I was approached and asked to usher. I agreed because I saw it as a way to be helpful and because I have the heart to serve. After a while of ushering, Anjala was very vocal and reminded me that while I was ushering and making sure everyone was greeted and taken care of, she was sitting with a two-year-old and twins who were four months old in a new church by herself. She wasn't saying it from a complaining place but that she needed help. Although serving in the church was a good thing, I failed to recognize the need to serve my family, and I decided to pause from serving as an usher until my children got older, and the burden on my wife was not as demanding.

Again, everyone is different, and I understand this chapter is likely to spark differing opinions. Remember, you are not married to anyone else but your spouse. You are not accountable to anyone else but your spouse. You don't owe an explanation to anyone else, and you should stay away from offering information about your marriage to every curious and nosy ear.

People make time for things that are important to them. There are 8,760 hours in a year, and if many of those hours are spent at work, church, on social media, hanging out with friends, etc., how can we expect our marriages and families to be built up? I enjoy spending time with my wife and family. We don't always agree, but we communicate in healthy ways that respect and honor each other. I trust her completely and confide in her with everything. I may communicate differently with her than I would a brother, but I don't stop communicating with her. She is me, and I am her. If I can't trust her, then I can't trust myself. Be intentional about spending more hours each year strengthening your marriage and family.

A quarter of 8,760 is 2,190, which is about ninety-one days or three months. Start now; don't wait until the new year to spend more intentional time strengthening your marriage. Turn off the devices and buy some board games, go on walks, have a family Bible study, camp in the backyard, take a road trip, write a book together, start a business, invest in a business, go to the pool, go play some sports together, get active, and do it together. It helps to develop habits of doing things together and enjoying each other's company. For some reading this, that is going to be a challenge because it is easy for you to be in the same house, and everyone is doing their own thing. We can look at our phones and technology more than we look at our spouses and children. Be intentional this year about making sure that is not you.

I like and love you

I like and love my wife. One thing I appreciate about the foundation of my marriage is that we were friends first. We became friends in college while working together and just enjoying hanging out with each other. We both were residential advisors (RAs) at the University of Michigan, and I can remember having to install bulletin boards in our residence halls every month. I worked in a residence hall with another RA, but Anjala had a residence hall she maintained by herself. I would help her brainstorm ideas and install her bulletin boards, and we supported each other. We watched movies together, studied together, and just enjoyed each other's company. We would be on the phone for hours until the sun would come up. I would fall asleep on the phone with her and wake up with the phone still there and ask if she was there, and I would hear her gently say, "Yeah, I'm still here." When we started dating and eventually got married, it just carried over.

Being friends helped us to like each other as individuals beyond intimacy. We talked and got to know each other, our likes and dislikes, good and bad; we trusted each other completely.

Jesus talks about the importance of building on a solid foundation. *Matthew 7:24–27 (NLT) says:*

> *Anyone who listens to my teaching and follows it is wise, like a person who builds a house on solid rock. Though the rain comes in torrents and the floodwaters rise and the winds beat against that house, it won't collapse because it is built on bedrock. But anyone who hears my teaching and doesn't obey it is foolish, like a person who builds a house on sand. When the rains and floods come and the winds beat against that house, it will collapse with a mighty crash.*

These verses remind me of our marriages. If the foundation you build upon are Jesus's words, wisdom, trust, friendship, and God, it will be strong and able to bear storms that will surely rise against you. If not, you are in for a shaky and unstable marriage. The interesting thing is you may not realize the house is unstable until it faces a storm. Both homes referenced in these verses function the same. They are mostly able to keep you safe and provide rest and security, but when storms arise, the strength and foundation of your love are tested.

Love will get you through a lifetime of partnership. It is a blessing to help someone on their path toward fulfilling the purpose of their lives. *Like* will get you through all the moments in between. *Love* is a journey of sacrifice, lows, highs, laughs, tears, joys, building, struggling, and overall fulfillment. *Like* is the difference in how you take the journey. It can determine if you take the scenic route and are able to enjoy the ride or if you are driving one hundred miles per hour the entire time just to get to where you are trying to go.

One of my favorite movies is *Click* with Adam Sandler. Adam Sandler plays a man who receives a remote control to control time and reality. The remote learns his behavior and learned to fast-forward through moments in life where there was about to be an argument or time spent doing something he didn't want to do, ultimately fast-forwarding him into the future. His wife marries someone else and so much more time and experience are lost. He missed so much time until he eventually died, having missed his family growing up.

> Loving and not liking someone is like fast-forwarding through time. You are just going through your marriage to get by, not really enjoying each moment.

Liking someone is not a requirement, but it certainly helps with spending a lifetime with someone if you enjoy their company. This upcoming year should be spent prioritizing your marriage and family so that you don't look up and realize life has passed you by.

Simple prayer: Father, thank you for allowing us to see this moment in life. You are faithful, even when we don't understand your perfect will. Help us intentionally build and seek you in our marriages and relationships each and every year. You are the source of our strength and the strength of our life. Help us be what you have called us to be and walk in our purpose this year. We need you and put all our trust in you alone. In Jesus's name, amen!

CHAPTER 6

Married into Forever

*For when the dead rise, they will neither
marry nor be given in marriage. In this respect
they will be like the angels in heaven.*

—Matthew 22:30 (NLT)

Retiring at forty

As you can tell by now, my wife and I are big on goal setting. We believe in planning for the future while making the most of the moment. One of the goals at the top of our list is retiring by forty. This is not kicking up our feet and doing nothing for the rest of our lives but no longer needing to work. It's being financially free and being positioned to live focused solely on building for God's kingdom and our self-identified goals and purposes. Do you have a *big* goal for your marriage? Is there a life-size desire or passion you both are focused on achieving? This goal should be bigger than just the hope of an upcoming event but something that shapes the disposition and behavior of decades of your marriage. This size goal should also be something that you all are not able to achieve individually or collectively without divine help. This is something you are constantly praying and seeking God for and something that not only God can do but something that will bring God all the praise and glory. If you do not have this life-size goal identified, take a moment to pray and reflect on what this could be.

Habakkuk 2:2 (KJV) tells us, "And the Lord answered me, and said, Write the vision, and make it plain upon tables, that he may run that readeth it." Having long-term goals in mind has helped motivate us toward achieving long-term and generational wealth, prosperity, health, and legacy for our family. Temporary goals are good but can be shortsighted. Have you set long-term goals for your marriage that give you hope to continue day-to-day, month to month, and year to year? Like the prophet Habakkuk said, are you taking the time to write down your vision and goals?

Most of us don't take the time to set goals or define our plans, so we live life very reactionally. When our lives get tough or frustrating, having the hope of retiring at the age of forty has been our marriage's subconscious and even conscious motivator and keeper. If you and your spouse have not identified a long-term goal for your marriage, please take the time to do so. Maybe it's starting a business, taking a sabbatical from work, doing a big project at home, or opening an orphanage together. There are limitless things you all can accomplish, but the important thing is, coming together in agreement to plan for these goals.

Am I really in love?

Two things have helped me in my fifteen years of marriage. The first thing that has helped me in my marriage is the power of knowing, being, and extending forgiveness. As stated in chapter 2 of this book, I have learned the power of forgiveness because I have needed it extended to me in my life. I have made decisions that were not the best and I often do now. I need the grace of God to help me through my life and help me to recover from negative and dark places. When I am bothered by something my spouse or someone else does, I may not immediately go to this place. But in reflection, I think of a time when I was in a need of forgiveness or grace. There was only one that walked perfectly on this earth, and everyone else will fall short of this mark. It is not about becoming a doormat for everyone to take advantage of your kindness or forgiveness but for you to grow in grace and wisdom knowing you are one decision away at any time from falling short of the mark.

My wife always says that she has low expectations for people. This is not a negative criticism centered on looking down at people or holding them to a standard they cannot live up to. It is simply acknowledging if *I expect less of you, I will not be disappointed if you don't deliver to my expectations.* As I mentioned before, I used to hold Anjala to such a high standard because she was my wife. I felt if anyone should know me, it should be her. In hindsight, those expectations were unrealistic and unfair. They led to Anjala never being able to live up consistently to my evolving personality and character changes. The troubling thing is she didn't even know it. You have to be careful with holding your spouse to unattainable expectations because some movie character or perfect ideal of marriage is defining marriage in a certain way.

It makes me ask, am I really in love with my spouse, or am I in love with the idea of loving my spouse? Am I in love with the house, family, jobs, and intimacy, but not the sick days, struggles, and sleepless nights? In America, we have a have-it-your-way mentality. You can literally go to a restaurant and pick and choose what you do or don't want on the menu. In other countries I have visited, asking to remove certain items from the food order can be considered an insult to the chef.

This is often how we treat marriage. We pick and choose what we do and don't like about it. When our marriage gets challenging or it is not what we envisioned it would be, we are ready to call it quits. That's why I keep repeating 1 Corinthians 13. This love standard is stronger, greater, and more perfect than any self-help book, movie, seminar, or counselor could ever provide.

The second thing that has helped me in my marriage has been consistent fasting and praying. My flesh always wants to say and do what it wants. It does not care what anybody else thinks or wants. It is the epitome of being self-centered. Have you ever been in a mood and tried your best to get out of the mood but could not? Fasting is withholding things from your flesh to weaken it and strengthen your spirit. Prayer is communicating with God by faith. Fasting and praying causes things that would not normally change to be released. The combination of them together can shake the very foundations of your marriage.

Anjala and I rarely make a major decision without both fasting and praying. As I previously mentioned, in 2021 our family committed to fasting and praying the first week of every month. As a family, we prayed that entire week and had Bible devotion. We committed to giving God the first part of every month. It was not easy, but the way God kept and blessed us during a global pandemic and so many other things was nothing short of supernatural. Imagine if you and your spouse come together with a similar commitment to God regarding your marriage? Maybe your situation is not desperate or on the brink of divorce; fasting and praying is not just a response to tragedy but a strategy for building a stronger relationship. *Matthew 18:20 (NIV) says, "For where two or three gather in my name, there am I with them."* There is power in individually doing these things, but when you come together to seek God through His Son Jesus, Jesus is present every time.

How can sin continue in the presence of Jesus? Abuse, adultery, alcoholism, gambling, sickness, stubbornness, you name it, and Jesus can remove it. All you have to do is decide in your minds that you are going to collectively come together fasting and praying to seek God! Forgiveness, fasting, and praying have been foundational in my marriage and family. I pray they will be a blessing in your marriage.

Let's build something together. (Lowe's 2006 marketing slogan)

In their book, *You and Me Forever*, husband and wife Francis and Lisa Chan discuss, how "marriage is great but it's not forever." They talk about being intentional about not allowing lesser things in life to destroy your marriage. These things cannot be a distraction from the greater things which are eternal. They speak on how marriage and intimacy in marriage were created to be enjoyed but should not take focus away from heaven. According to them, "It comes down to our focus. The way to have a great marriage is by not focusing on marriage."

Because of our busy lives, we often forget one component of being married. The busyness of life is temporary. Living focused solely on the day and task at hand can be a distraction and cause us to forget the life we will eventually live together and eternally with Christ. There is an eternal time we will all experience one day. This time will either be with Christ or without him. Something that helped me is understanding that although my wife and I will not be married when we make it to our forever season with God, we should still support each other today, positioning ourselves for success in forever. *Matthew 22:30 (NIV) says, "At the resurrection people will neither marry nor be given in marriage; they will be like the angels in heaven,"*

Our marriage should give God glory while on earth through helping others, supporting ministry efforts, living with integrity, loving your neighbor as you love yourself, raising your family in the fear of God, etc. This subtle shift in perspective has helped me love my wife, and I avoid *temporary arguments*, often caused by worrying and being anxious about the future and unknowns unnecessarily. The motivation for our actions should not solely focus on having treasure on earth at whatever the cost but having treasure in heaven. The Bible clearly talks about ways to receive rewards and succeed in the life to come.

> *Do not store up for yourselves treasures on earth, where moths and vermin destroy, and where thieves break in and steal. But store up for yourselves treasures in heaven, where moths and vermin do not destroy, and where thieves do not break in and steal. For where your treasure is, there your heart will be also. (Matthew 6:19–20 NIV)*

Whatever you do, work heartily, as for the Lord and not for men, knowing that from the Lord you will receive the inheritance as your reward. You are serving the Lord Christ. (Colossians 3:23–24 ESV)

Blessed is the man who remains steadfast under trial, for when he has stood the test he will receive the crown of life, which God has promised to those who love him. (James 1:12 ESV)

Anjala and I support each other's efforts toward strategically advancing God's kingdom. Yes, I say strategically advancing God's kingdom because the enemy is strategically trying to separate us from God and each other all the time. *First Peter 5:8 (ESV) states, "Be sober-minded; be watchful. Your adversary the devil prowls around like a roaring lion, seeking someone to devour."* The enemy will use envy, family, finances, friends, insecurity, jealousy, sex, social media, TV shows, work, and even the church to try to separate you and your spouse from supporting each other and ultimately being together. Since we know the enemy is seeking to devour us, we should not help him by being mad because of a difference of opinion or because of unhealthy communication. If your focus is *forever* and not *right now*, is what you are arguing about helping to build your marriage, family, or God's kingdom? Is that thought or feeling you can't let go of going to be the cause of stepping out of the purpose God has for you and your spouse?

I know it's hard to focus on storing up treasures in heaven when it feels like you are struggling to save them on earth. I admonish you to trust God and not focus on temporary arguments, stubbornness, and the pride of life that we miss the opportunity to build toward *forever* with our family and spouse in the life to come.

When I move you move, just like that.
(Lyrics from the song "Stand Up" by Chris Bridges aka Ludacris)

As I mentioned, my wife and I ironically met at a party at the University of Michigan. (Go Blue!) We had a great time and went from that party to another and then another. I could tell early on that we moved well together. We ended up connecting a year later and eventually became best friends. We were inseparable, supporting each other through classes, projects, and life. After graduating from college, we got married. I appreciate the foundation of our relationship was built on friendship. As friends, we developed agreement. ***Amos 3:3 (NIRV) tells us," Can two people walk together without agreeing on the direction?"*** This scripture seems simple, but my wife and I have counseled couples who are struggling in their marriages, and often it is because of disagreement. One spouse feels strongly about something, and since neither is willing to bend, there is usually a break over time.

As I have gotten older, some things are not worth being unmovable. Marriage is about sacrifice and being flexible. I am not telling anyone to compromise or not communicate how you feel, but keep in mind this is a race, not a sprint. In the past, I won arguments that cost me months or even years of emotional and mental repair in my marriage. Moving in the right direction takes patience and even compromise, but when you are moving together, it is a beautiful thing.

One of our favorite games to play together is a card game called spades. Spades is a partner card game of two players against two opposing players. It is a game of strategy where you are playing against your opponent physically and mentally. Anjala and I have learned how to play with each other over time and developed a skilled partnership. We rarely lose and when we do, it is usually because of me (insert shaking head emoji).

I have learned that moving in the right direction and in agreement with your spouse requires God. Are you keeping God in your marriage? When Anjala and I travel to unfamiliar places, we don't listen to each other regarding which way to go because neither one of us has ever been there. It would not be fair for me to be mad or hold it against Anjala for leading us in the wrong direction when I didn't know where I was going. This is what we do in our marriages. God alone knows the direction he would have us go, so why aren't we asking and trusting God collectively to guide, lead, keep, and direct our marriages?

Simple prayer: Father, we don't always know the direction to go in our marriages, but we trust in you completely. You know the thoughts and plans that you have for us, and they are thoughts of peace and not evil to bring us an expected end. Help us wait on you in our marriages to renew our strength. We believe in mounting up on wings as eagles and running and not being weary, walking and not fainting. Give us your direction even in the most chaotic storms of life, and help us to trust you completely. In Jesus's name, amen!

When spouses move in different directions, it may be frustrating at first, and over time, you will either get comfortable with moving separately or even start moving in the direction of someone else who is not your spouse. This, unfortunately, sounds like the norm for marriages today. This is a plan of the enemy. The enemy knows God has a purpose for your marriage. If God has called you both together, let no man or woman break you apart, even if that person is you.

Aligning with the direction God would have you go is critical for your marriage. It gives you purpose beyond today and helps keep you focused on things to come. If you are finding yourself getting comfortable with your spouse going in a different direction, ask God to help you break that comfort. The further apart you move away from each other, the longer it will take to come back together. Be intentional about stopping little things that don't align with your purpose before they grow into bigger concerns.

Luke 14:28 (NLT) says, "But don't begin until you count the cost. For who would begin construction of a building without first calculating the cost to see if there is enough money to finish it?" My wife and I recently went on a double date with a couple. The topic of purpose came up during the date, and I asked the couple if they feel as if they are walking in the purpose God has for their marriage. Are you in a marriage and have not asked God to reveal to you and your spouse His purpose. Your purpose is more than just going to work every day or having children, a dog, a house, and a white picket fence. There is so much more God wants you to accomplish, but you must agree. It is hard and challenging to be in a relationship with someone who disagrees with everything you do or say. Be flexible as you are headed toward where God would have you to be and intentional about inviting him into your marriage every day, month, and year of your lives!

Love never ends

My wife and I took a trip to Aruba for our fourteenth wedding anniversary. It was the best vacation I have ever been on. We had a blast. We went snorkeling for hours, taking videos and pictures of schools of fish underneath the ocean. We went parasailing for the first time—not once but twice! We jumped off a cliff into the ocean and went cave exploring. There were literally bats in the cave, and we immediately got out of there! We even went horseback riding on the beach. Now, neither of us is big on tourist attractions, so we went off the tourist path and ate at different local locations and food trucks across the island. It was beautiful, and I will never forget it. As beautiful as that trip was, it eventually came to an end. We said goodbye to Aruba and came back to America. The trip was refreshing and gave us a much-needed pick me up, but it did end. Most things that we experience in life will come to an end. We were not promised to live forever, but God's love toward us does not end.

This book reflects my life and collective experiences through these last fifteen years of marriage. Trust me, I do not have it figured out, but I understand it requires work and personal commitment. We've gone through highs and lows. God has been faithful in strengthening our communication through every trial, test, challenge, struggle, issue, heartache, setback—really *every moment* in our marriage. God has and continues to be faithful toward us! We now look at challenges as opportunities to grow, strengthen, improve, and love beyond the capacity we ever believed was possible. If you can apply 1 Corinthians 13 to your life, I believe this book will be helpful to somebody who is considering marriage, becoming engaged to be married, seeking to strengthen their marriage, or divorcing. I'm praying for each one of you because the enemy of this world is seeking to make a mockery of marriage, but that was not God's intent or plan. God's plan for marriage is for it to last until Christ returns or death do you part, and for those who have accepted Jesus as their personal Savior, you will be with God forever.

I struggled unnecessarily in my marriage early on, and in hindsight, I believe it is because I did not surrender everything completely to God. I would give God things I felt I could not do on my own. I would say, "God, I can take not being easily angered without you, so I need you to take care of my pride. God, I have temptation covered, and I just need you to handle the finances in our marriage. God, I am not arguing as much with my spouse as I used to, so I have that covered, no need to help me on that." This sounds weird but that's what I used to do unintentionally. I did not take everything to God. Now, no matter how small I think it may be, I ask God to help me navigate it all.

God's Holy Spirit has been invaluable in my marriage. Tugging at my heart and speaking to my spirit about what to do and not to do in my marriage. God's Spirit is promised to all those who accept Jesus as their personal Savior and choose to have a relationship with Him. **Romans 10:9 (NLT) states, "If you openly declare that Jesus is Lord and believe in your heart that God raised him from the dead, you will be saved."** It is that simple, and if you don't already, I invite you to have a relationship with Christ. Having a relationship with Jesus and choosing to be His disciple has truly kept my marriage, and I believe it will continue to keep us every moment, day, week, and year while married to my wife on this earth.

This book has been a labor of love. I hope that sharing my perspective and my own challenges, experiences, struggles, and trials have helped. Even for marriages that are strong and looking to sharpen your marriage and strengthen your love, I hope this continues to sharpen your perspective. Lastly, for both *singles* and those who are married and are seeking additional insight into the struggles, joy, partnership, and work required in creating lasting love, I hope this book has blessed you and provided perspective into what this marriage thing is about *outside of movies and popular culture.* I understand this book is not the answer to every situation because everyone's marriage is specific and unique, but I hope to encourage everybody to know you can grow together and truly deepen your love. Genuinely love each other moment by moment, day by day, week by week, month by month, and year by year, now and forever.

Simple prayer: Father, thank you for those who have taken the time to read this book. I pray you honor their seeking you in their relationships. As they put you first and seek to follow your guidance, I pray that it helps their marriage grow and flourish. No matter the situation, you have the power to turn and correct a situation we see as uncorrectable. You are the ultimate power with ultimate control. We trust you no matter what stage of our relationship or marriage. Help us to keep focus on eternity and not just the here and now. Bless each reader and get the glory out of their lives and help them to walk in their purpose as they trust you with all their hearts and not lean into their own understanding. In Jesus's name, amen!

Be blessed and know that you can make it in Jesus's name. I love you.

Marcus

ABOUT THE AUTHOR

Marcus Huff is a marriage coach and motivational speaker from Detroit, Michigan. He, along with his wife, led the marriage ministry for several years before becoming a youth leader. He has been featured on several relationship podcasts and panels. His passion for families also pours into his work as a community developer, developing black and brown communities across the country. A graduate of the University of Michigan, he and his wife have three children and live in Atlanta, Georgia.

Lightning Source UK Ltd.
Milton Keynes UK
UKHW012122030123
414772UK00001B/168

9 798886 165531